83-1199

DATE			

Strikes

Comparative Studies in
Social and Economic History 2

Strikes

Norman McCord

ST. MARTIN'S PRESS · NEW YORK

© Norman McCord 1980

HD
5365
.A6
M32
1980

All rights reserved. For information, write:
St. Martin's Press, Inc., 175 Fifth Avenue, New York, NY 10010
Printed in Great Britain
First published in the United States of America in 1980

Library of Congress Cataloging in Publication Data

McCord, Norman.
  Strikes.

  (Comparative studies in social and economic
history; 2)
  Bibliography: p. 129
  Includes index.
  1. Strikes and lockouts—Great Britain—
History. 2. Strikes and lockouts—United States
—History. I. Title. II. Series.
HD5365.A6M32 1980   331.89'29   80-52362
ISBN 0-312-76640-8

General Preface

Comparative Studies in Social and Economic History is a new series committed to the systematic examination of major historical themes in differing settings of time and place. All too frequently there has seemed to be no middle way between the learned monograph dealing with an historical episode in one narrow context and the more ambitious study generalizing at random from a bewilderingly wide-ranging background. Yet certain clear insights can be gained by a more controlled group of parallel and comparative studies. It is possible by means of concise individual *case studies* to underline those elements which are unique and particular to each topic's manifestation in a given time and place.

Each author in the present series will provide a framework for analysing a particular historical episode or problem in changing settings, and will also suggest a personal perspective in the opening and closing chapters.

Other comparisons published or in preparation consider the ideals and practice of urban planning in four different contexts, and the development of broadly-based municipal authorities in the Victorian city.

In the present inquiry Norman McCord examines, through the study of strikes between 1790 and 1970, the changing nature of industrial disputes in Britain and the United States.

J. R. Kellett

Contents

Acknowledgements

I am grateful to Dr A. J. Badger and Mr H. Harris for advice about industrial relations in America. For chapters four, five and six, I have drawn heavily on the principal published sources mentioned in the accompanying notes on further reading.

My thanks are due also to the general editor of this series, John R. Kellett, for helpful suggestions and to the publishers for their patience and forbearance during the writing of this book.

I am grateful also to Mr Frank Manders, who compiled the index and helped with proof correction.

Norman McCord

One

Introduction

The aim of this book is to offer to the student of history a number of examples of industrial disputes, together with some suggestions of sources for more extended study.

At first sight the subject of strikes may appear tolerably simple and straightforward, but in reality the theme is a very complex and varied one, offering problems and difficulties of understanding and interpretation. The development of industrial relations is not simply a question of social and economic history, but a matter of interest to many disciplines so that, for instance, it has implications for sociology, economics, political science, psychology and law. Each of these disciplines approaches the theme from the standpoint of its own particular needs, and the very large amount of published work in this field reflects the contributions to understanding derived from these different approaches. The object here, however, is not to consider strikes as a significant social phenomenon, but to examine a number of specific strikes as historical events and to try to draw from them some illumination of the historical context in which they occurred.

Even this limited aim encounters some of the difficulties of understanding and interpretation involved in studying industrial disputes, and the remainder of this introductory discussion concentrates on these problems. As has often been pointed out, it is very difficult, probably impossible, to establish a convincing common core of explanations for industrial disputes. Strikes and other forms of industrial conflict can occur from a very wide variety of different causes and exhibit a similarly wide variety in their development and duration.[1] The limited selection here necessarily omits some types of strikes of considerable interest, such as for example strikes arising from demarcation disputes, rival claims to specific work tasks fought out by competing groups of workers.[2] This kind of strike has caused considerable problems in certain industries, such as shipbuilding, but its overall frequency is not high. In a tabulation of 2,196 unofficial strikes in Britain during the years 1964–6 only fifty-seven could be attributed to this cause.[3] The limited group of individual strikes considered in the following chapters has been chosen on criteria which necessarily exclude many industrial disputes; the group includes strikes about which a good deal of evidence exists and which help to illustrate some distinctive features of the society in which they occurred.

THE SIGNIFICANCE OF STRIKES

It is however important to remember that the illumination which a study of strikes can offer is an inherently limited one. In the working of industrial relations a strike is an unusual event, and to study strikes by themselves touches upon only a small part of the complex pattern of industrial relations. It is important to stress this point, for we live in a context in which influential media of mass communications can present something of a distorted picture. Television, radio and newspapers are markedly selective in the items which they choose to present as news. There is an inherent bias, possibly an unavoidable one, towards an emphasis on events which are unusual rather than ordinary, and within this general tendency there is a strong appetite for things which have gone awry and embody such exciting strains as conflict and violence. It is not easy to make a compelling television programme or newspaper feature on a theme like 'Things carrying on as usual', but this may

[1] For an extended discussion of this point see, for instance, J. E. T. Eldridge, *Industrial Disputes* (London, 1968), especially chapters 1 and 2.
[2] *Ibid.*, 100–25, provides an extended discussion of demarcation disputes in one area of industry.
[3] Donovan Report, para. 820. (Report of the Royal Commission on Trade Unions and Employers' Associations, 1965–8. Chairman: The Rt. Hon. Lord Donovan. HMSO 1968.)

in reality have been a very common experience. A similar bias towards the unusual pervades a great deal of the evidence from earlier historical contexts. Newspapers have been with us for a long time and their selective contents have been much used as historical evidence. Reports from official enquiries of various kinds have provided another considerable mine of information, but they commonly reflect the same kind of bias towards the unusual and the disturbing; Royal Commissions and Select Committees are not in practice appointed to investigate the continuance of order and tranquillity, though these conditions may be widespread. Events which obtrude into our historical records are often abnormal events rather than events which are reliably representative of the normal behaviour of the society in which they occur.

In recent years it would be easy to conclude from the coverage of industrial relations in many elements of mass communications in Britain that our society is notably bedevilled by the problem of strikes. It has however often been pointed out that in the league of modern industrial societies Britain is usually somewhere in the middle of the table. Comparisons are not entirely easy, because of the variations in the ways in which different countries collect and produce the relevant statistics. Two official reports of the 1960 s do however give broadly reliable patterns. The Donovan Commission gathered evidence which was derived from a wide range of major industries for the years 1964–6; this showed that during those years Britain had 16.8 stoppages per 100,000 workers, while comparable figures were France 21.8, Italy 32.9, Sweden 0.5 and the USA 13.2.[4] Taking another approach, a government White Paper of 1969 presented data for the years 1963–7; the numbers of working days lost through stoppages per 1,000 workers were Britain 184, France 347, West Germany 34, Italy 1,045, Sweden 26, USA 934.[5] In general, Britain's strike record was worse than that of West Germany, Sweden and the Netherlands, but better than that of Australia, Canada, USA, Eire and Italy.[6]

This kind of general pattern does however conceal considerable variations within an overall national picture. Strikes are not in

[4] Donovan Report, para. 364.
[5] *In Place of Strife: A Policy for Industrial Relations*, HMSO 1969, Appendix 2, p. 38.
[6] Eldridge, *Industrial Disputes* (London, 1968), pp. 24–6. B. Aaron and K. W. Wedderburn, *Industrial Conflict* (London, 1972), chapter 2.

practice spread evenly, but occur in very varying incidence in different industries. Mining is an industry which has been notably strike-prone in many countries, and in the late 1960s one enquiry attributed one-third of all strikes in Britain to this single industry. Dockland provides another area in which stoppages have been unusually frequent, though many of them were brief. Between August 1977 and July 1978, for instance, dockers at Southampton were involved in eight short stoppages, while other groups of workers associated with the same docks were involved in another five stoppages.[7] Agriculture in contrast provides an area in which industrial stoppages have been very infrequent. It is possible for many workers to go through their working lives without being involved in any kind of strike. It should be remembered that a strike is not the only way in which workers can act to bring effective pressure to bear upon employers. An industrial dispute can be furthered by various forms of more limited action, such as a 'work to rule' in which production is severely limited by the rigid observance of rules which are tacitly ignored or modified in normal work practice. If the formal concept of a 'work to rule' has a distinctly modern ring, there have long been varieties of restriction on production which workers could employ to win concessions from employers. We should also remember that unemployment, industrial accidents and illness have caused the loss of many more working days than strike action.

It would be mistaken then to regard modern Britain as a country distinguished by a peculiarly bad strike record or one in which strikes have been an especially damaging feature of the society.[8] At the same time, a country with such a heavy dependence on levels of industrial efficiency and productivity is damaged by any factor which adversely effects these levels.

STRIKES IN A CHANGING SOCIETY

Industrial disputes, including strikes, have been a recurring feature of modern British history. It would, however, be a mistake to try to

[7] *Daily Telegraph*, 2 September 1978.
[8] For further discussion of this point see H. A. Turner, *Is Britain really Strike-prone? A Review of the Incidence, Character and Costs of Industrial Conflict* (Cambridge, 1968).

understand the history of industrial disputes in isolation. Instead, the development of industrial relations over the last couple of centuries or so must be seen against the background of a society involved in a complex and accelerating process of economic, social and political change. For example, the early strikes discussed in the next chapter occurred in the context of a Britain with a much smaller population, little formal government, and a pattern of small, locally orientated communities. It was a society in which gross inequalities of wealth, status, opportunity were the norm, as indeed they had always been in earlier times. The merchant seamen involved in these disputes were at the time unusual in the extent to which their strike action affected a much wider area, including the fuel supplies of the capital city. When we come later to the Pilkington strike at the beginning of the last decade, the context has been drastically transformed. A very much larger population was now predominantly urban, living in modern towns dependent upon an intricate web of interlocking services. Government had grown immensely, and now claimed a very considerable oversight and control of the working of the entire national economy. In many crucial ways local dependence had been replaced by national concepts, with the effectiveness of individual productive units now very much a part of a national level of performance directly affecting the standard of living of the community.

Concepts of society had also changed markedly, with a general acceptance of more democratic norms which would have astonished the Britain of 1800. Millions of workers were now organized in formal trade unions, and the trade union movement was already in 1970 one of the most powerful forces within the national community. Concepts of social responsibility had also altered markedly, with the development of the multiple attributes of the welfare state. This too could have a marked effect on the course of industrial disputes. When we come in a later chapter to the engineers' strikes of 1871, we shall find that a major preoccupation of the strike leaders was how to provide the necessary resources to support their followers. Consider the different situation obtaining during the strike of postal workers in 1971, which involved about 170,000 workers and lasted from 19th January to 8th March. The Post Office union had about £300,000 in its strike fund, and received £210,000 in grants and £356,000 in loans from other unions, while a public subscription brought in

£10,000. Most of the union's strike fund was spent in publishing propaganda in support of its claims. Workers without dependents were paid hardship benefits by the union, but strikers with dependents were expected to manage during the strike with the aid of public social benefits paid to their families.[9] The Poor Law of the nineteenth century had provided a less useful resource for strikers.

STRIKES AND THE LAW

While the course of industrial conflict has been much affected by the pervasive general changes in society, there are some elements which recur at many points in the history of industrial relations. One of these recurring strands has been the relationship between industrial conflicts and the public system of law. This too has seen changes of course. In many countries trade unions and strike action were proscribed until some time in the last century. In the context of the present century a right to collective organization by workers and a right to strike has been very widely recognized; this has sometimes been done in formal written constitutions, such as the Italian constitution of 1948 and the French constitution of 1958, both of which explicitly recognize a right to strike.[10] In Britain such constitutional enactments are not employed, but the effective change has been much the same.

There is a long history, however, of attempts to use the formal machinery of the law to control and regulate the conduct of industrial relations. It is, however, a difficult field for the law to seek to police, and the results have not always been happy, as was well exemplified by the brief existence of the British Industrial Relations Act of 1971. The failure of this attempt to regulate industrial relations by the use of legal sanctions was very far from unprecedented. The student of the recent history of this kind of legislation in Britain may well derive a wry satisfaction from an illuminating document emanating from a miners' strike of 1765.[11] Here a local magistrate is explaining to the central government why

---

[9] B. Aaron and K. W. Wedderburn, *Industrial Conflict* (London, 1972), p. 10.
[10] *Ibid.* pp. 55, 83.
[11] Public Record Office, S.P. 37/4.

he and his colleagues had thought it inexpedient to apply a recent Act of Parliament which had sought to give magistrates clear powers to intervene effectively in industrial disputes:

The Act beforementioned makes a provision upon the Information & complaint on oath of the Master, etc., for the Justice to examine and determine, & if the Servant be condemned, the Justice has a Power to commit the Servant to the House of Correction for a time not exceeding one Kalendar month; this is very well, where two or three or a dozen men desert their service, and has been many times properly executed with good effect, but when there is a general combination of all the Pitmen to the number of 4000, how can this measure take effect? In the first place it is difficult to be executed as to seizing the men, even if they shou'd not make a formidable resistance which scarce can be presumed, a few only can be taken, for upon the face of the thing it is obvious that the whole persons guilty can not be secured, so the punishment of probably 20 or 40 by a month's confinement in a House of Correction does not carry with it the least Appearance of Terror so as to induce the remaining part of so large a number to submit, & those men that shou'd be so confined wou'd be treated as Martyrs for the good Cause, and be supported and caressed, and at the end of the time brought home in Triumph, so no good wou'd arise, this I think not amiss to mention to your Lordship as a cogent reason for the Magistrates not proceeding on that Act . . .

Difficulties arising from attempts to apply legal penalties to problems of industrial relations have not been confined to such early contexts, and it appears that resort to the agency of the law does not present any simple or easy method of ensuring that the general public interest can be efficiently defended in the field of industrial disputes.

Another similar problem has arisen in connection with the question of picketing during industrial disputes. In Britain Parliament has made repeated attempts to provide a legal framework in this area, but it is a matter in which it is inherently difficult to provide the degree of precise definition of rights and wrongs needed for legislation, often even more difficult to apply the relevant law in confused and tense situations. It is possible that there would be a wide consensus in favour of strong legal penalties for spectacular and clear cases of brutally violent personal assaults during strikes, but to frame an adequate and effective definition of what is and what is not acceptable conduct on the picket line is not nearly so easy. Consider one of the key attempts which Parliament made to deal with this problem, in Section 2 of the 1906 Trade Disputes Act:

It shall be lawful for one or more persons, acting on their own behalf or on behalf of a trade union or of an individual employer or firm in contemplation or furtherance of a trade dispute, to attend at or near a house or plant . . . for the purpose of peacefully obtaining or communicating information, or of peacefully persuading any person to work or abstain from working.

It is not difficult to understand that the terminology employed here does not provide a precise yardstick by which picketing activities can invariably be assessed; for example, it is not easy to understand precisely where 'peacefully' ends and intimidation begins. This is, however, a very good example of the kind of problems facing legislators who try to employ the sanctions of the law in such a complex and basic area of human activity. The Liberal government of 1906 was not the first to try its hand at this task. The 1870s saw two celebrated attempts by successive governments—the Liberal Criminal Law Amendment Act of 1871 and the Conservative Conspiracy and Protection of Property Act of 1875—again with indifferent success. It is sometimes said that the former outlawed peaceful picketing and the latter allowed it; a more helpful summary would be that both governments tried to reach an adequate distinction between conduct which should and should not be permitted in picketing activities during an industrial dispute, but that both attempts were unsatisfactory because of the inherent difficulty of establishing legally effective criteria in this matter.

RIGHTS IN CONFLICT

A rather similar position has existed when a legislature has sought to deny certain specific rights, notably a right to strike in certain circumstances, to a particular group of workers, on the grounds that a public right to the continuance of certain vital services should be paramount over a right to strike. The two groups commonly affected here have been groups directly employed by the state in the administration of public business, and workers employed in certain vital public utility services. In the USA there has been a long history of attempts to enforce legislative restrictions on rights to strike by Federal or state officials. In most countries it is regarded as unreasonable to accept that the armed forces have a right to strike. In Britain the Conspiracy and Protection of Property Act of 1875 provided legal penalties against workers in the water and gas supply industries who interrupted these vital services by strike action, and an Act of 1919 added workers in the electricity supply industry to the list. Both in Britain and the USA it appears that this kind of punitive legislation has been ineffective in practice, and much of the British legislation has been a dead letter. There does remain, however, the point that it is by no means impossible that strike action can inflict serious hardship on the community, including society's weakest sectors; as yet, however, no effective answer seems to have been found to this considerable problem, which in some sense sees communal and sectional rights in conflict.

There is also a possible conflict of rights in another significant area. This is the long-argued question as to whether a right not to strike should be recognized as well as a right to strike, whether justice approves of sanctions being employed to prevent some workers weakening the effectiveness of strike action by continuing to go to work. Earlier legislation seeking to control and limit picketing practices was commonly influenced by a desire to provide legal protection for a worker who wanted to continue at work. Attempts to protect such workers, blacklegs from the strikers' point of view, have not been particularly successful. In Britain the overwhelming majority of trade unions have armed themselves with formidable disciplinary powers over their members which enable them to impose highly effective sanctions. In the principal engineering union, for instance:

any member who, in the opinion of his branch or the Executive Council, shall have injured or attempted to injure the union, or worked or acted contrary to the interests of the union or its members . . . may be expelled or otherwise dealt with by the Executive Council.

As some of the later chapters will illustrate, effective sanctions against blacklegs have not depended upon such formal provisions; there has been a very long tradition of intimidation and retaliation, and in this area of industrial relations bitter resentment can be held for a very long time.

A variety of arguments has been employed to justify this kind of collective coercion of dissentients. It has been suggested that workers who will enjoy advantages won by strenuous collective action—'free-riders'—are acting wrongly by refusing to participate in strike action or similar practices. For an interesting example of a different line of argument we may turn to Walter Reuther, one of the most prominent American trade union leaders of the mid-twentieth century. While testifying before a Congressional committee, he was asked by a senator whether he thought that a man who wanted to work had as much right to do so as a man who wanted to strike. Reuther's reply was as follows:[12]

I think (that) philosophically, I think that every member, every human being in a society has the same rights, the right to choose to go in, the right to choose not to go in, but I say that the human family was able to crawl out of the jungle of the past and build a civilization because we began to recognize that there are areas of human relationships in which somehow there has to be a social point of view in which the position and the problems of the group transcend the position of the individual.

Otherwise, we would all be living in caves yet, seeing who could get the biggest club to beat the other fellow's skull in. We got to the point where human civilization was possible only by recognizing that the total of the human family, whether it was a village or a state or a nation, and ultimately the world, that the whole of society has problems that we can resolve only by common decision, and that the individual has to be bound by those decisions. I think a worker who goes into a plant after a democratic decision has been made to strike the plant is wrong. He is morally wrong.

This is powerfully expressed, although it may not deal entirely with the libertarian argument which would support a right not to strike, for it is not entirely clear that a sectional group of strikers determined on strike action in pursuit of their own interests must be equated with the communal decision-taking of a family, village, state, nation or world community.

A further complication remains in considering the question of a right to strike. In Britain the last few generations have seen the elaboration of an increasingly sophisticated system of public

[12] W. E. Uphoff, *Kohler on Strike* (Boston, 1966), p. 279.

welfare services which collectively have emerged as a major source of employment. Ought strikes by workers in these areas to be regarded in precisely the same way as industrial action by workers in less sensitive fields? Recent decades have seen a considerable extension of trade unionism and militant industrial action in fields where these were rare or unknown at earlier periods, including the deliberate withdrawal of labour by groups directly concerned with the provision of welfare services to weaker sectors of society most in need of help. The year 1978, for instance, saw strike action taken by many professional social workers employed by local authorities, by ancillary workers involved in vital supporting services in a number of national health service hospitals, by workers in a charitable home serving very seriously ill patients. In all of these cases the industrial action taken involved deprivation and trouble to those in great need of help and support. Understandably the public response to these strikes was very far from enthusiastic, but the situation in such cases is rarely simple. Strikes do not normally occur in areas where harmonious industrial relations have been the norm in the recent past, but commonly represent the culmination of a period of frustration and dissatisfaction. Those involved in these disputes argue, with some reason, that it is impossible to have a satisfactory system of welfare services unless conditions are sufficiently attractive to recruit suitable personnel and unless those who work in such services are treated fairly and sympathetically. The particular difficulty arising in this kind of employment presents another instance of the way in which major changes in society's organization can affect the pattern of industrial relations and its implications.

IDEOLOGICAL IMPLICATIONS

It will already be reasonably plain that the question of industrial disputes is complex. Other complications for the student arise from another source. As with some other areas of social history, such as the history of poverty and the means taken to alleviate it, the history of industrial relations is a theme closely related to some of our own contemporary political and ideological preoccupations, and this can be a fruitful source of distortion and misunderstanding. This is not a particularly new situation, for strikes of the past have often had some sort of political implications, and these have varied.

The vast majority of strikes have been triggered off by issues directly related to practical down-to-earth problems of industrial organization—wages, conditions, restrictive practices, industrial discipline, a variety of personal relationships—rather than being sparked off by a strenuous concern with the wider problems of society as a whole. Political implications have sometimes become involved, however, in several ways. Some strikes have had an overtly political aim, as for example a brief strike in the London docks in 1920 which prevented the loading of arms on to a ship destined for Poland when that country was fighting Soviet Russia.[13] In Britain at least such overtly political strikes have been rare, and this has been the case in Western countries generally.

In other cases the existence of an industrial conflict may attract to the scene politically active groups who scent in the conflict an opportunity which is potentially capable of exploitation for their own wider purposes. In 1842 the radical Chartists sought to turn the 'Plug Plot', originally a spontaneous strike against wage reductions, into a general strike aimed at the democratic reconstruction of British political institutions.[14] In September 1978 the right wing *Daily Telegraph* was much concerned at the role played by a cell of Trotskyist university students in fomenting industrial conflict and sabotage in the Southampton Docks, including the especial impeding of trade concerned with South Africa.[15] Activities of this kind have certainly occurred periodically over a wide time span, but again they have not been anything like a dominant element in the course of industrial disputes in Britain. Another recurring situation is that in which the leaders of a strike may have a much higher degree of political interest and involvement than most of their followers; for example, John Burnett, leader of the engineers' strikes of 1871, had already appeared as a strenuous champion of parliamentary reform in the previous decade. Political involvement is not, however, something universally welcomed by workers actually engaged in industrial disputes, and it is certainly not unknown for outside support proffered by political

---

[13] A. Bullock, *The Life and Times of Ernest Bevin*, vol. 1 (London, 1960), pp. 133–4.

[14] J. T. Ward, *Chartism* (London, 1973), pp. 162–5.

[15] *Daily Telegraph*, 2 September 1978.

militants to be spurned by strikers who have judged such allies to be more of a liability than an asset to their cause.

Another form of apparent political implications may also be mentioned. In a variety of cases employers have deliberately fostered an impression that their recalcitrant workers were deeply imbued with subversive political motives. In industrial disputes of the late eighteenth and early nineteenth centuries, and the early Victorian Chartist years, it was not uncommon to find employers and their more militant friends claiming that the industrial action taken against them was something much more dangerous than that. The object was often to enlist official intervention against strikers. The ploy does not seem to have met with much success, and in many cases the claim of radical political involvement by strikers seems to have been either pure fabrication or wild exaggeration. A similar, if less unscrupulous, reaction can be found in employers who saw themselves as benignly paternalistic, and could not believe that their own workers would have come out on strike spontaneously. Such reactions have been seen in Britain, and also in other countries. During a strike by Boston carpenters in 1825 an employer protested:[16]

We cannot believe this project to have originated with any of the faithful and industrious sons of New England but are compelled to consider it an evil of foreign growth.

More than a century later it was still common to find employers in the USA employing private detectives to root out political subversion by outside agitators during strikes. In Britain too it seems likely that spontaneous actions arising from practical grievances at work have been far and away the most pervasive source of strike action, and that the work of political agitators has been very much more limited in effectiveness. In most strike situations it has been sufficiently clear that the workers involved did not require any kind of outside political stimulus to prod them into taking action to remedy their grievances.

There is another kind of political implication which should concern the student in this area of social history. Historical interpretations emanate from individual scholars who may well have

[16] W. E. Uphoff, *Kohler on Strike* (Boston, 1966), p. 131n. See also p. 36 for a similar reaction by an employer during the Kohler strike of 1934.

strong political and ideological preoccupations of their own. Indeed it would be a fair comment to say that those who choose to work in the field of social history commonly possess a degree of interest in political and ideological matters which is quite unrepresentative of society at large, and that these predispositions can have a very marked effect on the way in which historical topics are approached. In recent years the amount of valuable studies of industrial disputes available has increased very significantly, but the offerings have not always been well balanced. A high proportion of those drawn to this field exhibit a strong predisposition to sympathy for workers and a less happy approach to the task of appreciating the role of employers, managers and others with whom the workers may be in dispute. Yet for the competent student of history it is essential that he should try very hard to make the same effort to *understand* all participants in the situation with which he is concerned. The milieu into which an employer was born, and the influences to which he was actually exposed during his career, are important elements for this understanding, just as much as they are for any other participants. In many modern analyses of industrial disputes there has been a poorer level of appreciation of the ideas, interests, experience and aspirations of employers and managers than of the workers involved; here again more general changes in social concepts have affected approaches to questions of industrial relations. A kind of 'cowboys and Indians' approach, in which an industrial dispute is regarded with predisposed sympathies for one side, and predisposed antipathies towards the other, is frequently a recipe for deficient understanding.

Sometimes a lop-sided interpretation can result from a combination of political implications; this can happen where there have been political controversies involved in a certain historical context in ways which relate to continuing areas of political disagreement in subsequent years. Misunderstandings of this kind can often last for a very long time. Even in quite recent years, for instance, at various levels of education it has been common to find the Combination Laws of 1799–1800 regarded as legislation which crippled the development of early trade unions, or at least seriously hindered this. This is an interesting phenomenon, for it has in fact been known for nearly half a century that these Acts were generally ineffective and that little attempt was made by official authority to make them effective.[17] Another illuminating instance is provided by the case of the Tolpuddle Martyrs of 1834, in which six farm labourers in Dorset were sentenced to seven years' transportation to Australia after being convicted of administering illegal oaths in the course of trade union activities. A sustained protest campaign secured their release two years later. The case was of course real enough, but it is not so clear that the widespread use of this incident in subsequent interpretation as a reliable indicator of the nature of social relationships in the Britain of the 1830s ought to be upheld. If the transportation of workers for trade union activities was a typical event in that society it is somewhat odd that this single instance should have received such exceptional notoriety; and there is a good deal of evidence to suggest that the case of the Tolpuddle Martyrs was an exceptional and unusual event in that society, rather than a typical example of that society's normal mode of behaviour. It would be absurd to suggest that all studies of the history of industrial disputes have been impaired because of misconceptions inspired by powerful ideological commitments, but fair to suggest that this is a factor of which students should be well aware in a field in which such preconceived attitudes can be influential in shaping interpretations.

A PROBLEM OF EXPERIENCE

A further complication for the student to bear in mind is that history, including the history of industrial relations, is commonly written and studied by people who have little or no personal practical experience of the context with which they are concerned. Most studies of industrial disputes have been written by scholars, including the present author, who themselves have little or no actual experience of an ordinary working situation in industry, and whose training and modes of thinking can be very different from those of the people actually participating in industrial disputes. There is no way in which this situation can in practice be avoided, but it provides another limitation which should be borne in mind. There are particular problems of evidence involved in the study of

[17] D. George, 'The Combination Laws', *Economic History Review*, 1st Series, Vol. 6, (1935–6), pp. 172–8.

industrial disputes, in which many of those participating may be relatively inarticulate and a great deal can depend on feelings, moods and intricate personal relationships in an actual shop floor situation. The kind of evidence which would provide an adequate explanation of these factors, perhaps over a considerable time span, is often deficient, and it can be difficult to reconstruct these elements.

The brief account of the Pilkington dispute of 1970 given in a later chapter owes much to the valuable study of the strike, *Strike at Pilkingtons*, by Tony Lane and Kenneth Roberts. The authors of this book are university lecturers in social science, and their research on this topic was avowedly 'formulated . . . within the framework of social action theory'. The necessary imaginative jump from this intellectual posture to an appreciation of the ideas and attitudes of those actually involved in the strike required considerable dexterity, which is by no means lacking in the treatment. The problem of different perspectives, however, exists even in this meticulous study, exemplified in the authors' complaint that during the strike 'valuable opportunities were missed to experiment with forms of mass participation'.[18] It is unlikely that this kind of concept played any significant part in the strikers' thinking, but such comments can come naturally to scholars whose training and experience has taught them to think in such terms.

In writing about industrial disputes in which many individuals have been involved, historians necessarily have to use words of category and classification, for the treatment of all individuals concerned is obviously impossible. At the same time it is important to remember that the validity of some of these categories may be limited. In our society resort to such categories is commonplace and indeed unavoidable, but they ought not to be accepted uncritically. Such categories as students or old-age pensioners are perfectly valid for certain specific purposes. Classify someone as an old-age pensioner, for instance, and we know that an individual comes from a certain age bracket and is in receipt of a particular form of public benefit. Such classifying, however, only holds good for a distinctly limited purpose; it cannot tell us much about the character, interests, ideas and aspirations of an individual member of the category, nor can it tell us whether the individual concerned

[18] T. Lane and K. Roberts, *Strike at Pilkingtons* (London, 1971), pp. 18, 174.

is rich or poor, healthy or feeble, tolerably comfortable or in urgent need of help. So too when we know that a certain individual can be classified as a worker or an employer, this information tells us only a little about him. Human nature and human behaviour are complex and variable matters, and in dealing with industrial disputes, as with other areas of history, our resources for classification can often be far from wholly efficient. It is important not to place too rigid a reliance on the group words which have to be employed, and to remember that our groups will necessarily provide us with only very rough and ready categories; terms like 'the strikers' and 'the employers' may on many occasions conceal very wide disparities of temperament, ability and attitudes among the individuals of whom the group is composed.

With all these cautionary words we come to the collection of individual disputes. The sources on which these narrative chapters are based are mentioned in the notes appended to each; for the most part the accounts are based either on a limited range of published material or on primary sources unlikely to be available in practice to most users of this book. In these circumstances it seemed reasonable to omit detailed citation of references by means of a long series of footnotes in these chapters.

The first strikes discussed are two of the best-documented industrial disputes of the late eighteenth and early nineteenth centuries. There follows an account of an important mid-Victorian strike. The concentration on Britain is then briefly interrupted to provide comparative material in the shape of a summary account of three industrial disputes in America. The fifth chapter is devoted to a consideration of the 1926 General Strike in Britain, and the sixth to a significant dispute of 1970. This is followed by a final chapter which seeks to consider some general points arising out of the material assembled.

Two

Early Strikes

Two strikes by merchant seamen provide the earliest examples of industrial disputes to be studied here. One took place in 1792, the other in 1815. A main reason for the selection of these strikes to illustrate disputes of this period is that they are unusually well documented, but they are also significant for the light which they shed on contemporary social relationships. They are also especially useful in illustrating the way in which certain basic causes have lain at the root of many strikes over a very long period of time. The strike of 1792 arose essentially out of the perennial problem of maintaining standards of living in a period of sharply rising prices; the strike of 1815 arose essentially out of a problem of redundancy. In both cases the bulk of the men involved were employed in the great collier fleet plying between the ports of North-East England and London, which was one of the biggest elements in the British merchant navy at that time.

A number of circumstances facilitated the existence of effective collective action among the men employed in the collier fleet. The relatively short-haul trade with its uniform pattern of coal shipments provided ample opportunities for contacts and cohesion among the seamen concerned. Another factor here was the nature of the local seafaring communities; a high proportion of the families concerned lived in coherent local communities, often in their own sectors of the harbour towns, with their own patterns of culture and recreation within the highly localized communities of the day. The existence of this communal pattern with its own internal structures of influence and status was an important precondition for the very high quality of the leadership and organization contrived by the workers involved. This in itself provides an interesting indication that the development of the trade union movement did not necessarily provide cohesion among working groups previously devoid of capacity for organization; in some instances at least the coming of formal trade unionism could represent the creation of an institutional framework in place of an earlier informal pattern of influence and leadership.

THE 1792 STRIKE

In the late summer of 1792 rising prices faced the merchant seamen of the North-East ports with the prospect of a distinct fall in their standard of living unless they could obtain higher wages. A sympathetic naval officer put the situation succinctly in one of his reports to the Admiralty:

The Wages of the seamen of this port have not been encreased for a considerable time back since when the price of every article of living has encreased very much.

The normal method of payment in the collier fleet was a flat rate paid for each voyage to London. A figure of £2.10/- per voyage for able-bodied seamen had been normal for some time before 1792. As the year waned, and the prospect of longer and uncertain winter voyages approached, rising prices brought considerable unrest among the merchant seamen. In October their leaders brought before the shipowners a demand that the wages be increased to £3 per voyage for the six winter months November to April. At the same time the seamen acted collectively in a way which they had employed before to give point to their demands. They brought the coasting trade of the Tyne to a stop by enforcing the removal of the crews from all vessels in the harbour, and went on to complete the exercise by inducing or obliging the crews of ships entering the Tyne to come out also.

The reaction of the employers was also of a kind which has a long history. A shipowners' meeting held on 24th October considered the men's claim for a wage increase over the winter months, and refused the demand in the following terms:

It is fair and reasonable that the Sailors should receive a proper Satisfaction for the Toil and Dangers of the Service they perform, but extravagant Wages only produce Mischief to the Sailors themselves, by drawing to the Port a greater Number of Men than can find Employment, and by inducing more Persons to follow the Sea than the Trade of the Kingdom can receive: besides, such Wages cannot, in the Nature of Things, last long.

The employers' reaction was not wholly negative, however; they claimed in addition that they would have been very willing to consider a wage increase had not the men resorted to illegal and riotous measures by putting a forcible stop to the trade of the port. The shipowners argued, not very convincingly, that if they made concessions in such circumstances they might well be regarded as giving encouragement to tumult and disorder. A strong hint was given that if the men returned to their duty the shipowners would agree to a wage of £3 per voyage for the four months November to February.

The seamen had no intention of disarming themselves by abandoning their blockade before their demands were met: instead they announced that no coal ship would now be allowed to sail unless her owner agreed to pay four guineas per London voyage. They announced that vessels which accepted these terms were to fly a distinguishing flag, while the strikers effectively prevented the sailing of other colliers by maintaining a twenty-four hour guard of pickets on both sides of the harbour. Regular watches were organized, and seamen manned patrol boats to ensure that there were no unauthorized sailings. Favourable weather, and a buoyant demand in the London coal market induced some owners to submit to the men's inflated demands, and a few colliers duly sailed, amidst encouraging cheers from both banks of the river as they put to sea.

The bulk of the shipowners were not prepared to surrender to the men's demands. This spirit of resistance, as their letters make clear, was not due simply or primarily to unwillingness to pay their men an extra ten shillings a voyage over the six winter months, but much more to a deep-rooted determination to insist on the position of master and a blank refusal to accept coercion at the hands of their employees. Although there was never anything like a consistently united front on the part of the employers, a hard core of men in the Tyne shipping interest, mostly men in a fairly small way of business, believed firmly that to yield to the demands of the seamen was not simply to lose an industrial dispute, but to contribute to the overturning of that due subordination which was an essential element in the established order of society.

It is interesting to note, however, that this party of resistance had well-founded doubts as to how far their obstinate stand would be supported by official authority in the area. Three groups of local magistrates were potentially relevant to the dispute, and especially to the seamen's patently illegal blockade of the Tyne harbour. These were the magistrates of County Durham, Northumberland and Newcastle. The Durham magistracy was very weak on its northern Tyneside fringe, and the harbour town of South Shields had no magistrate who was normally in residence. The situation on the other side of the harbour, in South-East Northumberland, was nominally better, but the county magistrates there showed themselves distinctly reluctant to interfere against the seamen. The Newcastle magistrates were those most immediately involved, since their town enjoyed chartered rights conferring jurisdiction over the whole of the harbour area, but here again there was a distinct lack of eagerness for a fight. The trouble of 1792 was not by any means the first time that the Newcastle magistrates had been faced with trouble emerging from a major industrial dispute, and just as the seamen's blockade repeated earlier tactics, so the response of the Newcastle magistracy followed a dual line which had been adopted in the past, and was to be used again and again in the future. On the one hand the magistrates steadfastly refused to give any encouragement to the more recalcitrant shipowners, while on the other they sought the co-operation of central government and the armed forces so as to obtain a sufficient reserve of strength to preserve order in the event of any serious deterioration in the situation.

Two factors enabled the local magistrates to wriggle clear of the demands of the shipowners for the forcible breaking of the strikers' hold on the port. One was the understandable reluctance of most shipowners to proffer open accusations against the men's leaders backed by sworn evidence, for it was sufficiently clear that to act in this way might well expose the accusers to effective retaliation in future. Shipowning was a widely dispersed function, and many shipowners were people of moderate means who were themselves a part of the local communities of Tyneside. The shipowner who earned the strong enmity of the organized seamen might well live to regret such action in subsequent years. Moreover, the strike leaders arranged things so that, if effective physical pressure had to be applied to ensure compliance with the blockade orders, then the seamen directly involved were chosen from among those who were personally strangers to the owner and master of the ship involved.

The second factor which allowed the local authorities to remain quiescent was the very high level of discipline maintained by the strike leaders among their followers. The control of the *ad hoc* committee which led the seamen was firm, and these leaders were careful to avoid any serious outrages which might have alienated uncommitted public opinion or forced the local authorities to act decisively against the strikers. There was not much violence during the strike, and such violence as did occur seems to have been limited to relatively mild measures taken against seamen who in some way disobeyed the instructions of the strike committee. On a few occasions such men were carried through one of the local towns on a pole as a sign of ignominy; on 3rd November a shocked shipowner added to a letter of complaint addressed to the prime minister a postscript relating that a large crowd of strikers was at that moment driving naked through the town of North Shields a few sailors who had defied the regulations imposed by the seamen's leaders. However, there was a deliberate and skilful avoidance of any major provocations which could have forced the local authorities to intervene decisively against the seamen.

ATTEMPTS AT MEDIATION

At the beginning of November there were no signs of any weakening of the seamen's resolution, although the gradual build-up of naval and military units in the area was unmistakable. The commanders of these units were not, however, nonentities, but men of status and influence within that very unequal society, and they had ideas of their own about the dispute which were in conformity with those of most of the local magistrates. Certainly the officers of the army and the navy on the spot had no intention of acting as catspaws for the Tyne shipowners, and there is no good reason why they should have done so. A high proportion of the senior officers concerned were drawn from aristocratic sectors of society, in which traditions of paternalism towards dependents were deeply rooted, nor were they likely to be overawed by the very modest social status enjoyed by most of the local shipowners.

HMS *Racehorse* entered the Tyne towards the end of October and her captain, Leckey, at once joined the local magistrates in trying to bring about a mediated settlement of the dispute, an attitude which earned him the hostility of some of the hard core of shipowners. Leckey's intervention brought about a conference between representatives of the two sides in the dispute, held aboard *Racehorse* on 31st October. Clayton, the influential Town Clerk of Newcastle, attended in order to reinforce Leckey's attempts at mediation. The reaction of the two sides to the suggestion of such a conference is interesting. The seamen's leaders had expressed a willing and grateful acceptance of Leckey's invitation. The decision of the employers to take part in the meeting had only been reached after considerable disagreement and the decided opposition of an obstinate minority. Thomas Powditch was a member of this hard-core group. He was a shipowner on a small scale, and was to describe himself during this dispute as 'a person of more spirit than prudence'. Powditch thought the intervention of Captain Leckey 'very improper' and the speech in which he unsuccessfully urged his fellow-employers to boycott the proposed conference included the following trenchant statement of his views:

It is my opinion that Tampering with a Mob, treating with Rioters, or offering Terms to People illegally assembled for the purpose of extorting high wages from their employers, are crimes little inferior in magnitude to rioting itself.

It is significant, however, that the majority of his fellow-shipowners were not prepared to follow Powditch in this uncompromising resistance.

Leckey's intervention at the end of October failed to provide an agreed solution, and sparked off the dispatch to London of a series of letters from the party of resistance among the shipowners, complaining to the central government of the inaction of the local authorities. These complaints, however, were paralleled by the receipt by the central government of other reports, notably a series of letters from army and navy officers on the spot, which criticized the shipowners and argued that the seamen's grievances were well founded.

On 7th November the brig *Mary* attempted to sail from the Tyne. Her crew had signed ship's articles in the normal way, although this was something which the strike committee had forbidden for the time being, perhaps because this record might be used later as evidence that the men involved had participated in the enforced levying of higher wages on ships allowed to sail. A band of strikers boarded the brig, and tore out the pages concerned from the ship's articles. After second thoughts they returned a little later and made off with the whole book. This event caused a stir and a renewed flurry of activity by the local authorities, in response to immediate complaints from the shipping interest. On 8th November there was a meeting of magistrates from all three counties concerned—Durham, Northumberland and Newcastle. This meeting, however, flatly rejected the shipowners' demands that the authorities should use force against the seamen, and instead deputed one of their members, Rowland Burdon, to make another attempt at mediation. Burdon was a paternalistic Tory magistrate, a Member of Parliament, a well-known figure in coal and shipping circles, and a man who seems to have enjoyed a genuine local popularity. The decision to ask him to mediate was taken with the encouragement of the army and navy officers who had been present during the magistrates' discussions.

Before seeking a meeting with the strike leaders Burdon managed to wring from the shipowners an agreement to offer the higher wage of £3 per London voyage for the period October to March. The seamen's leaders, while careful to express their appreciation of Burdon's efforts, held out for the payment of the higher wage until April, since October 1792 was now well past. Not all things were going well for the strikers, however; they could not be blind to the continuing build-up of naval and military forces in the area, and on 11th November they learned that the Admiralty had declined to take any action on a petition the seamen had submitted in support of their case.

However, the Royal Navy's part in the dispute was not to become a merely negative one. On the evening of 15th November, just after the failure of Burdon's first attempt at mediation, the naval forces in the Tyne were reinforced by the arrival of the frigate HMS *Hind*. Her commander, Captain the Hon. Alexander Cochrane, took over the role of senior naval officer on the spot. He was to show himself a man of humanitarian and liberal views as well as a cool and sensible observer. During his present commission he had already shown that he shared the generous sympathies of his more famous nephew, Thomas Cochrane, 10th Earl of Dundonald. The elder Cochrane had been appointed in *Hind* to the Leith station primarily for anti-smuggling operations, but he had signalled his arrival there in January 1791 by promptly ending a series of disgraceful abuses in the treatment of sick seamen on that station, with the Admiralty's full approval. More recently, in the summer of 1792, he had received the formal thanks of both Edinburgh Corporation and the Admiralty for the part he had played in composing local disputes in Edinburgh.

Like other naval and military officers involved in police duties in this period, Cochrane regarded police work as an unwelcome necessity, distracting him and his colleagues from their proper functions, and often arising from ineptitude or neglect of duty on the part of civil authorities. Cochrane's ship was badly in need of a refit after a strenuous commission, and to add to his concern she grounded heavily on the Tyne bar while entering the harbour. Cochrane was under orders to proceed to Sheerness as soon as possible, and was anxious to get his ship into dockyard hands. He was therefore anxious to see an end to the seamen's dispute, but showed no inclination towards a forcible solution. His reports to both the Admiralty and the Secretary of State were admirably impartial, and he soon came to have a poor opinion of the part played by some of the shipowners. In one letter to a cabinet minister he wrote of 'the Owners whom I am sorry to say that the sailors have but too much reason to complain of'. He found ample evidence that some of the more unscrupulous owners had often cheated their seamen in the past, and duly transmitted these reports to the central government. By mid-November he possessed a powerful squadron of ships and a substantial force of marines, sufficient to have enabled him to break the strikers' blockade of the Tyne had he chosen to do so. Instead, however, he threw all his influence behind a second attempt at mediation by Burdon, while his reports to London emphasized his impressions of the orderly and non-violent attitude of the strikers.

TERMS OF SETTLEMENT

Early on 19th November a group of magistrates, including Burdon, with Cochrane's strong support, succeeded in wringing from the shipowners some further concessions. Later that day Burdon carried the new terms to a meeting with the strike leaders at South Shields. A prolonged conference ensued, during which Burdon made it clear that, if these new terms were refused, the authorities would have no choice but to use the forces at their disposal to free the harbour. Finally agreement was reached; the terms included the higher wage rate being paid until May, and promises by the owners to improve conditions on board, including the supply of food. In addition Burdon promised that he would take an early opportunity to bring before Parliament a Bill to set up a statutory wages board for the merchant marine, with representation for both seamen and shipowners and with powers to fix wage rates. With this agreement of 19th November, this strike by the North-East seamen came to an end.

In a report to the central government on 21st November the senior army officer on the spot, Colonel Delancey, expressed the strong opinion that if the employers had acted sensibly from the beginning, all the trouble and diversion of army and navy units would have been unnecessary. One of the local newspapers, the Whig *Newcastle Chronicle*, regaled its readers on 2nd December with an account of an incident during the strike. When HMS *Martin* arrived in the Tyne to join the security forces she grounded heavily, and her crew were unable to extricate her from the shoal. She was thereupon rescued by the strikers, who despatched groups of boats to haul her off. The *Chronicle* reported the meeting on board *Martin* between her captain, Duff, and the leader of the rescue force, who was reported as saying, 'We know well enough, by God, Captain, what you've come about, but, damn it, we'll save His Majesty's ship for all that.' It is unlikely that this incident was merely imagined.

Burdon tried to bring his scheme for a statutory wages board before Parliament but had no success; although an honest and well-meaning man, and an important figure locally, he was no great parliamentary orator, and his plan collapsed in face of the cold reception accorded it by Pitt's government and the strenuous opposition mounted by the shipping interest.

The strike by merchant seamen was paralleled by similar efforts by other groups of workers to obtain increased wages in face of rising prices, with mixed results. Miners in north Durham obtained only minor concessions, but those in Northumberland won more. Strikes in the coal mines of the North-East dragged on until February 1793, when the Mayor of Newcastle could report to the central government thankfully that:

The exertions of the Gentlemen concerned in the Coal Trade accompanied with some Compliance on the Score of Wages have in a considerable Degree appeased the Colliers.

The merchant seamen's strike of 1792 provided illuminating information on the nature of social relationships in Britain at that time. The strike of the same body of workers in 1815 is even more illuminating, and in that case the evidence is fuller.

THE 1815 STRIKE

In the summer of 1815 the end of the Napoleonic War saw extensive demobilization of the government's maritime resources. The greater part of the operational ships was paid off, as was the great mass of hired shipping which had been operated by the government's transport services during the war in such functions as supplying the campaigns in Spain or the allied army in the Netherlands during the Waterloo campaign. This rapid demobilization caused widespread unemployment among merchant seamen and consequent industrial disputes in various ports. The late summer of 1815 saw moves by unemployed seamen to obtain redress of their grievances in the Port of London, the Clyde, Leith, Hull and Yarmouth, but far and away the most impressive demonstrations took place in those North-East ports which were the centre of the East coast coal trade.

The first hint of serious trouble came in mid-August, with a move by local seamen to obtain the expulsion from local ships of foreign sailors who had been recruited during the wartime shortage of seamen. There were a number of cases of the forcible removal of foreign seamen from local ships, and at the same time the local seamen collectively put forward to the magistrates at Newcastle a demand that no foreign seamen should be employed in local ships while local sailors were out of work. The term 'foreign' was sometimes used ambiguously, and there was even strong resentment at the employment of Yorkshire seamen in Tyne ships while Tyneside sailors were out of work. In reply to the demand for the expulsion of foreign seamen, the Newcastle authorities replied that they had no power to do any such thing, but that they would transmit the petition to the central government with a supporting letter. The Mayor of Newcastle duly did this, writing to the Admiralty to confirm reports of distress among seamen and their families and to express the hope that something would be done to remedy this situation. Another passage in his letter of 14th August was however of a different tenor, reflecting the duality of approach we have already seen in 1792. The Mayor requested the despatch of a warship to the Tyne, as without such aid the local magistrates would find it impossible to exercise their authority in the harbour areas if the seamen should turn to drastic action in support of their demands. The Admiralty showed no inclination to respond to this request. In earlier disputes the Admiralty had concluded that large-scale and unwelcome naval involvement had been caused by the failure of local authorities to intervene decisively at an early stage, and it seems clear that there was sympathy in the Royal Navy for the grievances of the seamen and no enthusiasm to play a part in their forcible suppression. Avoiding a blank refusal, the Admiralty temporized, telling the Mayor that nothing could be done until a suitable vessel was manned and available on the much reduced peace establishment of the Navy. At the same time the Admiralty did try to help, by ordering the last commander of the navy's wartime impressment system on the Tyne, Captain Caulfield, to re-open his office for large-scale recruiting into the peacetime navy, with the added sweetener that volunteers taking advantage of this facility would be allowed to select the ship in which they were to serve. A plaintive reminder from Newcastle's Mayor that the stationing of a naval force in the Tyne had been of great value during the last demobilization period fell upon deaf ears at the Admiralty.

THE ORIGINS OF THE DISPUTE

During the next few weeks the number of unemployed seamen on Tyneside, and their resentment, mounted. Their complaints against the shipowners were well founded. During the war, partly because of the operations of the navy's press gangs, owners had been operating with smaller crews but had been forced to give much higher wages than had prevailed in peacetime. Now that the war was over, many shipowners were trying to keep the small wartime crews while at the same time exploiting the great pool of unemployed seamen to drive wages down. This attempt to have it both ways on the part of the employers was bitterly resented by the seamen, and resulted in the emergence among the sailors of a remarkable demonstration of unity and skill in defence of their interests.

Early in September an *ad hoc* committee representing the seamen of the Tyne presented local shipowners with a list of demands. The demand for the exclusion of foreign seamen from local ships was repeated, but the two most important claims were those which related to wages and crew size. On the river Wear a parallel approach faced the Sunderland shipowners with equivalent demands. The wage claim was for a Tyneside figure of £5 per London voyage with, as was normal, a slightly lower figure for the Wear trade. In January 1815 the wartime wage rates had been running as high as £8 or £9. On both rivers the wage claims were in fact moderate, and these demands were conceded by the owners without much trouble. The seamen's second main demand was for the public acceptance by the shipowners of a fixed and definite ratio of crew size to tonnage. There was ample evidence of ships sailing short-handed while many seamen lacked employment. Moreover, many of the seamen concerned had recent experience of the government's transport service, which did operate with a fixed ratio of manning to tonnage. The seamen expressed the hope that Parliament would act to make such a ratio compulsory on all British shipping, but in the meantime the demand of the North-East seamen was that the owners should accept a scale of five men and a boy per hundred tons. It was this demand which lay behind the 1815 strike.

The seamen's claims were presented to the shipowners on 7th September, but the men had already begun to act to give point to their demands by bringing the trade of the port to a stop. No local coasting vessel was allowed to sail after 4th September, and this embargo was again enforced by large and well-organized groups of seamen, who went off in boats to any ship which began to weigh anchor, or otherwise prepare for sailing, and obliged her crew to desist and go ashore. From the beginning, however, the strike committee in charge of the men's side of the dispute was willing to compromise in certain cases. A ship whose owner accepted the men's demands might be allowed to sail in return for a donation to strike funds. By the end of the first week in September both of the principal harbours of North-East England, as well as smaller local ports such as Blyth, were very much under the control of the seamen's organization.

The shipowners also set up an *ad hoc* committee to represent their interests during the dispute. On 7th September this committee met to discuss the men's demands and resolved

1st. That the Proposition of the Sailors for Manning the Ships employed in the Coal-Trade, the same as when in the Transport Service, cannot be complied with.
2nd. That in order to afford relief to the Seamen, it is the determination of the Meeting, to give the preference to those who have served their time out of, or are at present resident Householders in the Port, and as long as any such are out of employment, no Stranger can be employed.
3rd. That the Wages shall be for the Summer Six Months, say from 1st. April to the 1st. of October four Pounds per Voyage, and for the Winter Six Months five Pounds per Voyage.

The owners were not completely inflexible on the subject of crew size. They refused any general ratio of manning to tonnage, but put forward the alternative suggestion that each local ship should be inspected by members of the committees of the local marine insurance companies, who would be empowered to fix a suitable figure for crew size for each vessel.

The next day saw a number of developments. The seamen sought to gain support for their case by despatching a respectful and well-argued petition to the Admiralty asking for help from that quarter. Three of the seamen's leaders took this document to the senior naval officer available, Captain Caulfield, and asked him to transmit it to the Admiralty on their behalf. Caulfield agreed to do so and warned the deputation that they should be very careful to avoid any violence in the conduct of the dispute. Throughout the prolonged strike Caulfield was sending to London balanced and sensible accounts in which he repeatedly stressed the general orderly behaviour of the strikers. The seamen's petition bore 780 names, 490 of whom signed their own names, while the marks of the remainder were properly witnessed.

The owners also met on 8th September, and determined on a formal approach to the Newcastle magistrates, urging them to do their duty, open the port and break the seamen's patently illegal blockade. As in 1792 this approach by the shipowners received a distinctly cool response from the local magistrates. The Mayor of Newcastle flatly refused to intervene in the dispute unless he was provided with clear evidence of violent behaviour by the strikers. The Mayor was, however, privately stepping up his pressure on the central government for the supply of reinforcements in case the situation did turn ugly. The army was disposed to be helpful, and on 13th September Major-General Riall agreed to order to the scene the bulk of the small forces he had immediately available, three out of his four troops of the 5th Dragoon Guards. He also told the Mayor that he intended to accompany this force himself. The Navy was much less forthcoming. When the Mayor repeated his plea for naval support the Admiralty replied on 13th September that:

their Lordships must decline to take such a Step which would lead to the Employment of a Military Force in a Case which appears to my Lords to belong to the Civil Power.

A further pleading letter from the Mayor on 16th September pointed out that, though the matter concerned the civil power, that power could not effectively act in the harbour without naval support; this evoked from the Admiralty the advice that if the forces available to the civil power were inadequate he should address himself to the Home Office. The Navy was obviously very reluctant to become involved in this dispute.

LOCAL ATTITUDES

Meanwhile the shipowners met again on 9th September, when it became clear that the men were not going to accept the offered terms. The owners edged their offer upwards a little by dropping their proposed seasonal differential, and accepting the men's original claim for £5 per London voyage throughout the year. The owners were, however, adamant in their refusal to accept a fixed ratio for manning and proffered the argument that if they were forced to face higher costs in this way trade would be lost and the end result would be less rather than more employment for local seamen, not a line of argument likely to be very convincing in the circumstances. At the same time the owners repeated their demand to the local magistrates for the forcible ending of the blockade of the Tyne, a demand again rebuffed by the Newcastle authorities.

On 15th September the Admiralty reply to the seamen's petition reached Caulfield and he handed it over to the strike leaders. It came as a distinct disappointment, for the Admiralty would go no further than repeat its offers of large-scale voluntary recruitment for the peacetime Navy. Caulfield reported to the Admiralty that he had duly handed over the reply and added:

I took the opportunity of again impressing on the minds of these men, the danger, as well as folly of their proceedings—and they repeated their promise, that no act of violence should be committed—which I have every reason to believe as about 6000 of them walked thro' the Town this day, and quietly dispersed.

The failure of the petition to the Admiralty did not lead to a disposition to surrender on the men's part, and the owners now tried another tack to bring official resources to their aid. Having failed to elicit any help from the Newcastle magistrates, the owners' committee arranged for a meeting of local magistrates from the Northumberland and Durham benches. This produced no helpful result either, for these magistrates effectively refused to intervene, and confined themselves to advising the employers to publicize their case more. Despite repeated approaches by the employers, local magistrates showed an unmistakable reluctance to come to the owners' aid in a dispute in which there was certainly a good deal of local sympathy for the seamen.

This sympathy, clear from other sources, is not very evident from the local press. The Tory *Newcastle Courant* was from the beginning virulently hostile to the strike, and repeatedly accused the strikers of responsibility for acts of violence unsubstantiated in any other source. The Whig *Newcastle Chronicle* took a more moderate line, criticizing the strikers more in sorrow than in anger, and especially stressing the way in which the strike threatened the livelihood of other groups of workers, such as the coalminers. Of all the local newspapers the reaction of the radical *Tyne Mercury* is particularly illuminating. This was the most sprightly and readable of all the local journals of this date, but despite its undoubted political radicalism it showed itself from the beginning in uncompromising opposition to the strike. The *Mercury* may have been very keen on parliamentary reform, but it was equally keen on the maintenance of sound orthodox concepts of political economy, and the seamen's combination and demands for restrictive practices in manning were anathema to the *Mercury*'s radical proprietors. A series of editorials expressed an offensively patronizing tone towards the seamen which they particularly resented, and there ensued a paper war of handbill and editorial in which the strike leaders gave as good as they got—the strikers even took advertising space in the *Mercury* to air their disagreements with the paper's policy.

While continuing to avoid any commitment to come to the aid of the shipowners, the Newcastle magistrates were understandably alarmed at the continuing stoppage. On 22nd September the Mayor despatched to the Home Secretary, Lord Sidmouth, a lengthy account of his earlier attempts to obtain support from the armed forces, and especially asked Sidmouth to exert pressure on the Admiralty for the provision of a naval force. Major-General Riall had furnished a force of 160 troopers with which to back up the area's tiny police resources and local militia and yeomanry units, but without armed boats and marines the magistrates would be at a serious disadvantage if the seamen's strike turned ugly. However, all of this official correspondence about raising armed strength remained confidential and was not communicated to the shipowners. The Sunderland magistrates were adopting a similar course of action too, giving no public countenance to the employers' resistance while privately concerned about the possible dangers involved in a continuance of the strike. On 26th September Riall provided the Sunderland magistrates with a detachment from his tiny force in response to the magistrates' urging.

The Home Office duly responded by exerting pressure on the Admiralty, and on 27th September Sidmouth wrote to tell the

Mayor that a twenty-gun ship had been ordered to the Tyne. The Admiralty had yielded grudgingly, however, and had ordered the ship's captain not to intervene actively against the strikers. The Admiralty's distaste for involvement in the affair may not have been the only reason, for there were expressions at the time of doubts as to how far the naval seamen might be relied upon to act effectively against other seamen.

On 28th September the town of Newcastle was treated to a demonstration of the strength and organization of the striking seamen. A large procession of seamen wound its way through the town, escorting a number of their fellows who had disobeyed the orders of the strike leaders. These victims were paraded with their faces blacked and their jackets reversed as an object lesson for others and a target for derision. Depositions made at the time by eye-witnesses described an unofficial trial of similar defaulters at North Shields, which resulted in the rough handling of those accused of disobedience. On the whole though, this kind of reprisal appears to have been limited to comparatively innocuous measures.

Another deposition made at the time by an eye-witness is valuable because it gives us a glimpse of the strike committee in operation. William Coppin, a shipowner, described his experiences when he visited the public house which was the committee's headquarters in order to seek permission to send one of his ships to sea. While he was present a seaman came in and asked for help, as he had been unemployed for some time and was in distress. The record books were produced and the committee granted him five shillings, with a hint to be careful with it as funds were not plentiful. Coppin also heard the committee give orders for the overnight imprisonment of a crew and a pilot who had evinced a disposition to get a vessel to sea in defiance of the blockade. When Coppin's own application was heard, it was supported by a committee member who had been an apprentice on one of Coppin's ships. After some hesitation his request was granted, on certain conditions; a printed counterfoil book was thereupon produced and the necessary passport entered in duplicate in this printed form. Coppin received one copy as his evidence of permission to sail his ship, the other was retained for the information of the pickets.

October opened with the North-East ports still paralysed, and no obvious end of the dispute in sight. Despite the favour he had already received from the strike committee, William Coppin tried to send another ship, the *Joseph*, to sea without permission, using no seamen, but a scratch crew of masters and apprentices. As soon as her anchor began to move, groups of seamen put out in boats and forced their way on board. After a lengthy altercation Coppin was obliged to give up his attempt to sail. This incident produced a further meeting of the shipowners' committee later on the same day, 2nd October, and the exasperated employers determined to force the hands of the Newcastle magistrates to put an end to this kind of illegal interference. A formal memorial, signed by forty-three shipowners, was sent to the Mayor, requesting action to maintain law and order in the harbour. In view of an Act of Parliament of 1793 specifically passed against the forcible detention of ships—a measure not unconnected with the strike of 1792 already considered—the actions of the seamen in 1815 were patently illegal, and the formal memorial from the owners made it difficult for the magistrates to maintain their position of neutrality. However, the Newcastle magistrates were still not prepared to break the strike at the behest of the employers, and their only reaction to the memorial was to inform the owners that the magistrates had decided to intervene as mediators, since attempts to settle the dispute by negotiations between owners and seamen seemed to have failed. The magistrates still refused to apply force, though by this time they were receiving strong hints from the central government too that the illegal stoppage had gone on for too long and that the rule of law ought to be vindicated.

On 4th October the Mayor and other Newcastle magistrates came down to the harbour in state with a view to mediation. This attitude was obviously resented by the owners, who were distinctly cool during their meeting with the magistrates. After this uncomfortable meeting, the magistrates received a deputation of strike leaders, and subsequently made it clear that they agreed with the seamen that there ought to be a parliamentary regulation of manning levels. The Mayor tried to persuade the owners' committee to agree in the meantime to the issue of a scale of manning on the lines suggested by the seamen. Despite this clear indication of the magistrates' view, the owners remained obdurate and refused to budge on this issue, while reiterating their willingness to see crews fixed by the local marine insurance bodies.

The owners responded to the disappointing response of the magistrates by holding a mass meeting of the Tyne shipping interest on 7th October. A manifesto putting forward the owners' case emanated from this meeting; this document included a calculation that acceptance of the owners' scheme for crew fixing would add on average two men per vessel to existing crews. This was not an entirely fortunate admission, since it was obviously tantamount to accepting the seamen's claim that ships were in practice under-manned. Certainly the seamen were not in the least overawed by the employers' manifesto, for they replied to it by publishing a squib of their own, the *Seamen's Chronicle*, which provided in mock-Biblical language a parody of the shipowners' general meeting of 7th October and its proceedings. Part of it went as follows:

6. Know ye not Brethren that if we accede to the claims of these *pestilent seditious fellows*, we shall be under the necessity of drinking at least one Bottle of wine per day less than our usual Beverage.
7. And I would ask, Who among you are willing to do this? Rather than submit to such a privation, perish the seamen from the face of the earth!
8. Verily, brethren, does not your sleek skins, your *port*-able bellies, and the colour of your noses, inform me that you prefer your bottle to any feelings of humanity; yea, to any consideration whatever.

This sprightly piece went on to a slashing attack on the editor of the radical *Tyne Mercury* for his opposition to the strike, and ended

15. But none of these things moved the Seamen, but they continued their meetings as formerly, and found favor in the eyes of all the people.
16. And those who possessed any portion of a certain quality or ingredient called humanity; and all those who had the welfare and interest of their Country at heart, wished them complete success.

In addition the strikers embarked upon a series of naval demon-strations in the Tyne, manoeuvring large formations of boats in obedience to flag signals.

THE CENTRAL GOVERNMENT'S ROLE

In London the Home Office was the recipient of a varied range of correspondence from the North-East about the lengthy dispute, ranging from angry complaints from the blockaded shipowners to more balanced accounts from naval and military authorities on the spot. The Home Secretary, Lord Sidmouth, was naturally worried about the long duration of this patently illegal action by the seamen, and dubious about the failure of the local authorities to intervene decisively to maintain law and order within the area for which they were responsible. Sidmouth decided that he needed some reliable information about what actually was happening in the North-East ports, and therefore despatched to the area an emissary of his own, who was to provide confidential information from the scene of the dispute. For this role Sidmouth selected John Cartwright, a county magistrate from south Durham and a Tory paternalist. The Home Secretary briefed this agent on 12th October, and Cartwright duly arrived on Tyneside on 14th, sending off his first report that same evening. These reports from Cartwright are extraordinarily interesting documents. The first, written immediately after the emissary's arrival on the scene, includes little which might seem unexpected, consisting largely of criticisms of the seamen's effrontery in taking the law into their own hands. Cartwright did however pay tribute to the solidity and coherence of the men's organization, and their orderly behaviour; he also noted that 'They have quietly and civilly collected a good deal of money among all classes'.

After three days' experience on the spot a significant change can be seen in the second long report which Cartwright sent to Lord Sidmouth. His assessment of the situation, and the responsibility for the dispute, had markedly shifted:

As a disinterested stranger, I have been in crowds of seamen, heard their complaints, views and intentions, and witnessed their proceedings—and, setting aside the absolutely intolerable violence and illegality of the power they have assumed to restrain the trade and business of the ports, I feel myself compelled to bear my testimony to your Lordship in favor of their principles, and in other respects good conduct, as well as the solidity of their grounds of complaint . . . Ships from these ports have gone to sea shamefully deficient in strength to navigate them, and should this subject ever excite the attention of the legislature, hundreds of cases may be produced, in which avarice has risked at sea a helpless insufficient crew, in a crazy *but highly insured* ship . . . Your Lordship has too much humanity, to fix an eye exclusively on the crime these poor men are committing in search of redress, without giving some consideration to the circumstances out of which that crime has arisen.

Cartwright enclosed for Sidmouth's information details of one particularly glaring case of a local ship which had sailed to America and back with an obviously inadequate crew. He then went on to give his opinion of the employers involved in the dispute:

I found my way yesterday to a public table at Sunderland, where except myself all were shipowners. I heard a full discussion of the subject. They openly, to my deep disgust, avowed the base dissimulation with which they are acting and that they intend to observe any terms they may *agree* to only till the present compact association and consequent danger are dispersed. The unprincipled avarice, and want of integrity in this class of men as a body, appears to be one reason for the bias observable in favor of the seamen, perhaps too of the *negligence of the Magistrates*.

The middle of October saw further attempts at mediation on both Tyne and Wear. On the former river these negotiations failed to bring about a settlement, but things went differently at Sunderland. There both sides to the dispute agreed to call in a well-respected county magistrate as mediator; the Reverend William Nesfield, JP, Rector of Brancepeth, was, like Rowland Burdon, a prominent local figure with a long record of arbitration in industrial disputes which stretched back at least as far as the 1790s. Nesfield embarked in mid-October on a prolonged and patient course of negotiation with both seamen and shipowners on the Wear which finally brought about an agreed solution to the manning problem in that port on 21st October.

On the Tyne the dispute was not to end so tranquilly. On 17th October the shipowners' committee, exasperated at the prolonged refusal of the local magistrates to free the port, drafted a long formal memorial to the Home Secretary, reciting a full history of the dispute from the employers' point of view and complaining bitterly of the inaction of the local authorities.

Meanwhile Lord Sidmouth was himself concerned at the way in which the seamen were being allowed to flout the law week after week. He believed that the local magistrates should do their duty and that they now had ample force to vindicate their authority. On 19th October Sidmouth issued definitive orders to the Lords Lieutenant of Northumberland and Durham, and the Mayor of Newcastle, instructing them to bring to an end the illegal stoppage of the ports. Sidmouth's view was that the law must be obeyed, but that legitimate grievances certainly ought to be remedied:

When the conduct of these persons shall in this respect be changed, their representations and complaints ought and I trust will be heard with attention and indulgence, and that consideration and liberality shewn to them which is due to British seamen.

Obedient to Sidmouth's categorical orders, the magistrates of the three counties issued a declaration on 20th October, condemning the continuance of the blockade and expressing the view that the terms offered earlier by the employers should now be accepted. When the men made no response, the authorities at last acted to open the port of Tyne. A skilfully planned and executed police action took the heart out of the opposition with very little difficulty. Early in the morning of 21st October there was a sudden swoop by naval seamen and marines which seized the boats on which the strikers depended for their control of the harbour, and at the same time troops moved into the riverside towns to seal off approaches to the harbour. Faced with this decisive intervention, mass meetings of the Tyne seamen decided to call of the strike and return to work on the wage and manning terms offered by the employers earlier.

The response of the owners' committee was to try to use the intervention of the authorities as an opportunity to water down the concessions they had already offered; this was greeted with a chorus of exasperated anger from both magistrates and army and navy officers which obliged the owners at a meeting on 23rd October to stick to the terms they had offered. By the evening of 22nd October a number of laden ships had sailed from both Tyne and Wear, and the long dispute was essentially over on terms which gave the seamen many of the demands they had originally made in early September. Some of the most belligerent employers would have been glad to see extensive reprisals against strike leaders, but their desire for revenge was substantially thwarted by the reluctance of both central and local government to embark upon such a campaign. Sidmouth repeatedly informed local authorities that there should be no prosecutions, except for men who could be seen to be guilty of either personal violence or the deliberate destruction of property, and he time and again urged mildness on local magistrates. A few seamen were arraigned early in 1816, and seven were sentenced to terms of imprisonment ranging from two to twelve months—scarcely draconian in view of the general nature of the contemporary penal code. In all of these cases the defendants were accused of direct participation in violence. In general the reluctance of the Home Secretary and the local magistrates to participate in any kind of witch-hunt after the event was unmistakable.

CHARACTERISTICS OF THE STRIKE

One of the most obvious features of the whole story of the 1815 strike was the very remarkable degree of restraint and moderation displayed on almost every side. The seamen evolved an extremely effective organization which was allowed to control the North-East ports for some six weeks, and did so with very little violence, as all reliable witnesses agreed in testifying. Magistrates, army and navy officers, and the Home Secretary, Lord Sidmouth, were slow to initiate drastic action against a patently illegal blockade, and markedly unsympathetic to any display of intransigence on the part of employers. Even the shipowners themselves were prepared to offer considerable concessions in response to the men's demands on pay and manning, and the strike ended with a pay increase and a compromise system of fixing the scale of manning for local ships.

Another feature of this interesting dispute is its limited nature. This is a notably well-documented example of an early nineteenth-century strike and the evidence demonstrates the absence of any wider political significance behind the dispute. The notable organization of the seamen was deployed in support of certain specific trade demands, and the strike seems completely devoid of any association with contemporary radical demands for political reform. An official agent on the spot told Sidmouth after the strike was over that:

it does not appear that the Seamen had any other object in view beyond that which they averred which was an increase in wages and that the Ships should carry an additional number of men in proportion to their tonnage.

On 6th October, at the height of the dispute, another Cartwright had appeared on the scene; the veteran radical reformer, Major Cartwright, addressed a meeting in Newcastle on the subject of parliamentary reform. The strikers seem to have taken no interest in his visit, and the seamen's strike was not mentioned in any of the press reports of this radical meeting. We have already seen how the orthodox radical newspaper, the *Tyne Mercury*, was hostile to the strike, so this lack of contact between industrial action and radical politics is scarcely surprising, and it was not rare in early nineteenth-century Britain.

Alike in 1792 and 1815 these strikes by merchant seamen demonstrated a remarkable capacity for skilful leadership and organization among the men concerned. Examples of the sophistication involved have already occurred in the earlier narrative, but another instance from the 1815 strike may help to clinch the point. When Lord Sidmouth's emissary, John Cartwright, was travelling north to pursue his enquiry, he observed an interesting incident at a point ten miles south of Sunderland. A mail coach travelling south was examined by a party of three seamen, representing the Wearside strike committee; a seaman among the passengers was obliged to produce the pass issued by the committee to authorize his departure from the port, while the investigating trio 'seem'd in their turn to think it necessary to account for themselves and produce their vouchers'.

It would not be easy to find a greater degree of organizational skill in such matters among any other contemporary group of workers. It is worth noting that these skills were deployed at that time in defence of a tightly knit sectional interest rather than any wider concept of social class. Both in 1792 and 1815 there is little evidence of any effective co-operation between the striking seamen and other groups of workers within the region affected. The seamen's strikes could bring serious problems for other groups of workers involved in the coal trade, such as the miners and the keelmen, but this does not seem to have resulted in significant co-operation. It would be wrong to see in these events a conflict between two broad social classes, for neither the propertied groups in the area nor the workers exhibited anything like a united front. The strikers appear to have enjoyed considerable sympathy and even support from the dominant minority groups in contemporary society, while there is no evidence to suggest that the seamen received any substantial backing from other groups of workers. Similarly, during the major strikes by North-East coalminers in 1831–2, the seamen preferred to safeguard their own interests rather than come out in support of the miners. This is not to deny that much wider sympathies have been evident in the course of many other industrial disputes. Some industrial disputes have been fought on a distinctly narrow front, while others have engaged the attention of broader sectors of society.

Three

The Engineers' Strikes of 1871

The year 1871 saw a strike among engineering workers which was one of the most significant industrial disputes of nineteenth-century Britain. This strike succeeded in enforcing a reduction in the length of the basic working week in that industry, and marked an important stage in the long-drawn-out campaign for the reduction of hours of work generally. The engineering workers of North-East England were far from being the first in the field in the cause of reduced working hours, but the prominence of the 1871 dispute gave a major stimulus to such efforts and a significant example to engineering workers in other regions, and indeed to workers in a variety of other trades. Moreover this 1871 strike has a more general significance in the history of industrial relations in Britain, for it was taken on every hand as being something more than a local industrial dispute about hours of work. Instead it came to be regarded as a major confrontation, embodying such basic opposed conceptions as the right of employers to untrammelled freedom of action in operating the businesses they owned, and the right of the workmen to ensure that their interests received due consideration in decisions taken by employers in the conduct of their business.

BACKGROUND TO THE DISPUTE

In the 1850s and 1860s, as the engineering industry of North-East England expanded rapidly, there had been earlier attempts to limit the length of the basic working week, as well as efforts to obtain other kinds of concession from the engineering employers. The fortunes of these attempts normally varied with the prevailing economic situation. When trade and profits were booming, and when the threat of strike action was especially unwelcome to employers, concessions of various kinds could be gained by the workers, but when trade was slack and the prospect of profits appeared bleak, employer reaction tended to stiffen. These factors can be seen at work in the immediate background to the 1871 dispute. Pressure for better conditions had mounted during prosperous years up to the mid-1860s, but in the recession of the later years of the decade collective pressure by the workers fell away. Those years saw commercial set-backs and some notable bankruptcies among local engineering firms, paralleled by wage cuts and unemployment among engineering workers. When, however, in 1870 the economic scene brightened markedly, there was an immediate resumption of pressure by the engineering workers. The first fruit of these altered circumstances was a successful campaign to substitute weekly for fortnightly pays in the engineering industry of North-East England. This was a gain of considerable benefit in practice for the men, though the way in which it was forced on the employers by collective action seems to have aroused in some of them a determination that the prerogatives of the employer must be defended against future attacks, and a rooted unwillingness to knuckle under on any other issues.

The basic working week in the North-East engineering trade was fifty-nine hours; the major disputes of 1871 centred on a demand from the workers that this be replaced by a fifty-four-hour week, to be gained by reducing each of the five main working days from ten to nine hours. The campaign for this objective began late in March with a relatively brief conflict on Wearside. The decision to press for a shorter working week was taken mainly on tactical grounds. When the leaders of the Wearside engineering workers held their first meeting on 22nd March 1871 they could have chosen to fight for a straight wage increase, which could probably have been won fairly easily in the existing boom conditions in the industry. There were however precedents for the decision to press for the fifty-four-hour week; there had been earlier attempts to gain this concession in the engineering industry, and the fifty-four-hour week had already been won by some other groups of workers. The shorter working week possessed other advantages over a simple pay claim. If the campaign should lead to a serious dispute, the fight for shorter hours was one which could be made appealing to un-committed public opinion. It could be argued that the men were campaigning for a shorter working week for a variety of edifying purposes, and that the extra hours would be employed by the engineering workers in a number of improving ways, such as caring for the health and education of themselves and their families. Since only a tiny proportion of the engineering workers in North-East England were trade union members, it was highly desirable to fix upon an objective which could be relied on to elicit sympathy and support from other sectors of society.

We need not take too seriously the repeated claim that a shorter working week would naturally lead to the use of the extra five hours in a variety of edifying and healthy ways. The idyllic picture of the engineering workers in general devoting this time to the education, culture and health of their families was a useful propaganda point, and may well have been accurate in some cases, but acute critics pointed out that a reduction in the basic working week could in practice lead many men to work much the same hours as before, but with a higher proportion of them paid at higher overtime rates. Another crucial advantage conferred by selection of the hours issue rather than a straight wage claim was that effective action by workers in the engineering industry could be seriously impaired by the existence of fratricidal rivalries be-tween men of different trades and different levels of skill. A claim for a shorter week might hope to avoid these internecine conflicts by bringing what appeared to be similar benefits to everyone concerned. The hours claim therefore represented well-chosen ground for the engineering workers in the spring of 1871.

Both on Wearside and Tyneside there was available a high quality of leadership well able to appreciate the tactical op-portunities of the situation. If less than a quarter of the skilled engineering workers were trade union members, there was an important nucleus of influential men who were keen union members. There can be no doubt, however, that the significance of this nucleus in the major disputes of 1871 derived not from their possession of trade union office, but from their own individual prestige and qualities of leadership. Like other groups of workers anywhere, the engineering workers of 1871 were not simply amorphous masses, but societies with their own structures of influence and prestige. The existence of a pattern of leadership within groups of workers did not wait upon the organization of formal trade unionism, but existed earlier in the shape of informal authority exercised by men who were individually influential among their fellows.

THE STRIKERS' AND EMPLOYERS' LEADERSHIP

During the strike on Wearside in March and April 1871, which acted as a curtain-raiser to the main struggle, Andrew Gourley emerged as the most prominent leader among the Sunderland engineering workers. He was a keen trade unionist himself, who had worked on Tyneside during the early 1860s and made a name for himself as a workers' leader. He had already championed the idea of fighting for a shorter working week, but when lean times came in the later 1860s the position of an outspoken leader was not very comfortable and Gourley found it expedient to migrate to the Wear. In the next few years his capacity as a leader manifested itself again; due very largely to his efforts the Sunderland Branch of the Amalgamated Society of Engineers grew from 140 members in 1866 to 330 in 1870, though the latter figure still represented the enrolment of only a small proportion of the workers eligible to join the ASE.

Under Gourley's influence the Wearside engineering workers decided on 22nd March to select the shorter working week as the target to be aimed at. The decision—as with all the major decisions in these strikes of 1871—was taken by the representatives of the skilled tradesmen, and although many labourers were affected by the dispute they exercised no effective influence over the control of the workers' side of the conflict. The strikes which developed first on Wearside and then on Tyneside were controlled by *ad hoc* committees of the leaders of the skilled engineering trades, and on both North-East rivers the men's side of the disputes was managed with considerable dexterity.

On the last day of March the Wearside engineering employers returned a flat refusal to the request for a fifty-four-hour week put forward by the men's committee, and the men's leaders called their followers out on strike early in April. Both parties to the dispute sought to enlist support from their brethren elsewhere, and it appears that in real terms the men received more effective help and encouragement than the Wearside employers. The Wearside engineering industry was less firmly established than that of Tyneside, and on Wearside no really outstanding leadership emerged among the employers. The attempt to establish and maintain a common front even among the engineering works in that restricted area proved a dismal failure. Breakaway concessions by individual firms anxious not to lose the boom conditions prevailing paved the way for general surrender, and by 5th May the Wearside men were back at work with the fifty-four-hour basic week conceded. This result represented a rapid and conclusive victory for Gourley and his associates, a local collective leadership which had remained firmly in the saddle throughout the affair. The Wearside dispute had seen one interesting minor brush, when William Allan and Robert Austin of the national ASE headquarters had arrived on the scene with the intention of taking over the conduct of the dispute; this attempted intervention from outside had however been hotly resented by the Wearside strikers. Allan and Austin received a distinctly lukewarm reception. The local leadership retained its full control of the men's side of the dispute.

Meanwhile in the course of April, developments on Tyneside led up to a much more strenuous conflict. Here too the spring of 1871 brought unmistakable improvement in the economic position of the engineering industry, and renewed agitation among the workers to follow up the earlier victory on weekly pays secured by the beginning of the year. It was not until a month after the Wearside move on the hours issue, however, that action of a similar kind was taken on Tyneside. On 22nd April a meeting of delegates from Tyneside engineering works decided that they too would press for the fifty-four-hour week. It was noticeable, however, that the references to employers at this meeting were couched in respectful terms, while a number of the men speaking expressed a willingness to see the matter taken to arbitration. In the last days of April the men set about the organization of their campaign for the nine-hour day, and here again the key leadership was provided by an *ad hoc* committee representing the genuine leadership in the various works.

On Monday 29th April a delegate meeting at the Westgate Inn, Newcastle, which was the men's headquarters throughout the strike, formally established the campaign as the Nine Hours-League—a title with echoes of the struggles for free trade and parliamentary reform. The informal committee now enjoyed the grandiose title of 'The Acting Committee of the Nine Hours League'—'acting' here being used in the sense of active or managing rather than provisional. With one exception we know tantalizingly little about the men who formed this committee, yet they undoubtedly represented a genuine workers' leadership always present to some degree, but now emerging for a few months more fully into the limelight of publicity. We need not suppose, however, that it was the immediate crisis which made these men influential among their fellows; the committee merely mobilized for the course of the dispute a pattern of shop floor influence which already existed.

In one important instance we do know more than a name, and this is the man who was the main spokesman and most prominent leader of the strike of 1871 on Tyneside. John Burnett was born at Alnwick, Northumberland on 21st June 1842, and he was educated in The Duke's School in that town. Orphaned when he was twelve, he moved to live with an uncle on Tyneside. For two years he worked as an errand boy, and then at fourteen entered a local engineering works as an apprentice. In early manhood he rapidly established a reputation for high intelligence and capacity for leadership. With Andrew Gourley he emerged as one of the men's leaders at Palmer's works in the 1860s, and like Gourley he found it expedient to move from Palmer's during the lean years of the later 1860s, though Burnett only moved up-river to Armstrong's works at Elswick. In addition to his qualities as a shop floor leader Burnett was a prominent member of the Newcastle Mechanics' Institute, and also played a part in the local parliamentary reform campaign of the mid-1860s, an experience which brought him useful friends and contacts among leading Tyneside Liberals.

Burnett was a man with marked gifts as a leader and organizer. He was fully alive to the abilities and the claims of the workers he championed, yet throughout his career he preferred methods of conciliation and negotiation to outright conflict in industrial disputes. He was never a revolutionary, but believed that in Britain any attempt at violent change would be less healthy and less fruitful than co-operation between the workers and the more enlightened sectors of the groups which already possessed power. He retained a belief that substantial improvements were to be gained by working within the existing structure of society. In 1871 he was to face a very tough struggle, but it is worth remembering that this strike of 1871 was fought in the context of a society which only a few years before had conceded that political rights should be extended to many workers, and a society in which revolutionary groups were marked primarily by their impotence and remoteness from the major developments of the day. In viewing society in this way Burnett was certainly not an isolated figure among local workers' leaders. Thomas Burt and William Crawford of the coalminers were men of similar stamp, and it is not surprising that the area's miners were to contribute generously to the movement led by Burnett in 1871.

With the formal establishment of the Nine Hours League at the end of April 1871 Burnett became its President, and he drafted the message in which the League respectfully asked the Tyneside engineering employers for the shorter basic week. Warned by the earlier episode on Wearside, the Tyneside employers had anticipated their workers' demand, and most of them were determined to resist it. The majority of the Tyneside employers proved capable of a greater degree of co-operation than their Wearside counterparts had evinced. Moreover, in Sir William Armstrong the Tyneside masters possessed a leader notable for his own personal prestige and for his qualities of strong-mindedness and determination. From the beginning Armstrong emerged as the keystone of the opposition to the Nine Hours League, and counted on the support of the majority of his fellow engineering employers on Tyneside.

One firm in which recent changes provided Armstrong with more vigorous support than he might otherwise have obtained was the old-established one of R. & W. Hawthorn. Robert and William Hawthorn were brothers who had built up a major engineering enterprise which had been marked by good industrial relations and a continuing tradition of paternalism. However, Robert Hawthorn had died in 1867 and in 1870 his brother William sold out to new proprietors. These new men were concerned to vindicate their authority and determined to ensure that the business continued profitable. The new senior partner, Benjamin Browne, was a thirty-two-year-old civil engineer who had sunk all his personal resources into the firm as well as borrowing heavily to facilitate the purchase.

His principal partner was F. C. Marshall, an interesting figure in the dispute as a major employer who had worked his way up from the shop floor. He had already established something of a reputation as a tough employer, and was to be one of the men's most adamant opponents during the 1871 dispute.

To the engineering employers who enrolled under Armstrong's banner in 1871 the demand for a shorter working week was in itself dangerous, for to them it threatened to raise labour costs and by doing so undermine the competitive position of their works. More than this, however, to surrender to a league of workmen on an issue like this was to jeopardize the prerogatives of an employer to operate his business as he saw fit. It was perfectly possible for someone like Armstrong to recognize that when skilled labour was in short supply a workman might well be able to obtain better terms from masters competing for his services, but this was a very different matter from a league of workers presuming to lay down rules as to the number of hours a factory might work. To Armstrong, possessed of a strong sense of his own position, resistance to the men's demand was understandable. In a quarter of a century he had seen the Armstrong works grow under his direction to become one of the greatest engineering establishments of the day, giving employment to nearly three thousand men. It was natural for Armstrong to arrogate the credit for this achievement to his own enterprise, managerial skill and capacity for technical innovation. It was equally natural that he should resent attempted dictation from workers whose achievements were so patently inferior to his own, who were to him primarily the beneficiaries of his own achievements.

Armstrong was very willing to take the lead in resisting the pressure of the Nine Hours League, and the employers' side of the dispute was largely administered by the team of key managers which Armstrong had recruited for his Elswick works, including Andrew Noble and the two Rendel Brothers, George and Stuart. The majority of the Tyneside engineering employers lined up behind Armstrong and opposed to the Nine Hours League their own *ad hoc* grouping, the Associated Employers. This body received the men's claim for a shorter working week on 2nd May, and a few days later replied to it with a blank rejection. In addition to the refusal of the men's demand, the employers' reply was couched in a form which was in itself offensive in manner. The men had specifically asked for direct negotiations, but the employers refused to accept the Nine Hours League and instead sent their reply in the form of a letter from a firm of lawyers; there was no disposition on the part of the employers to accept the League as a recognized negotiating body. In refusing any direct contact with the League, the associated employers were already displaying the intransigence which marked their attitude for most of the long period of conflict.

The employers were not, however, entirely united in this uncompromising front, and events in two major engineering enterprises on Tyneside showed that there was no single concept of industrial relations within local industry. George Robert Stephenson and Charles Mark Palmer showed themselves to be much more skilful and conciliatory. They both showed themselves unwilling to accept the shorter basic working week, but instead of the bleak rejection of the associated employers they talked things over with their own workers and exerted their own personal prestige among them, with the result that these two major engineering firms were not affected by the strike which followed.

THE COURSE OF THE STRIKE

After the original rejection by the employers, the League's committee called a special meeting for Saturday 12th May to discuss what should be done next. At that meeting there was predictable criticism of the employers' impersonal mode of replying to the men's first proposition, but strong majority support for another respectful and conciliatory appproach, aimed at asking the employers to reconsider. Accordingly another respectful letter was drafted and sent to the employers, asking again for direct negotiations. Burnett and his principal colleagues had throughout urged the importance of maintaining an appearance of patience and sweet reasonableness, but on Tuesday 15th May the men at one of the local firms jumped the gun, coming out on strike against the wishes of the League's leaders. The employers promptly used this overt act to refuse any further contact with the League; and Burnett and the other leaders of the workers, while angrily criticizing the men who had forced their hand by coming out prematurely, could only respond by calling out the remainder of their followers. Before the end of May some 7,500 men were on strike, facing the League with its biggest problem, how to arrange for the support of the men and their families.

The workers were not, however, without valuable allies in the conflict. Probably their most important single friend was Joseph Cowen, an important local industrialist, politician and proprietor of the *Newcastle Chronicle*, a skilfully-managed newspaper then rising to a prominent place in the expanding provincial press. The *Chronicle* gave the League continual press support of great value in ensuing months, while Cowen himself contributed not only helpful information and advice but also financial backing which was of crucial significance in the early part of the strike period. Burnett and Cowen had already come together in local Liberal politics and were able to co-operate very closely during the 1871 strike.

Two examples will illustrate the nature of this useful link. On one occasion Cowen's own contacts informed him of an attempted breakaway from the Nine Hours League, and he at once passed on to Burnett details of the intended meeting for that purpose. That meeting, so Cowen's biographer tells us

had been arranged for that night, by a party of workmen with outside friends, and its object was to concert plans for a return to work. Thanks to the friendly hint, some of the nine-hours leaders attended the meeting— which was designed to break up their movement—and owing to the representations then made, were able to prevent any serious results.

It would be pleasant to know more about the actual nature of these 'representations'! On another occasion Cowen offered Burnett a personal gift of money to help him during the strike. Burnett refused in the following terms:

he told him that he was almost afraid to go out in the suit then on his back, because, during a strike, men grew so suspicious that they would say almost anything against a leader who was too well dressed.

Even before the strike took place there were attempts to forestall the stoppage by some kind of mediation. The first attempt of this kind was made by the Mayor of Newcastle, the moderate Liberal and businessman R. B. Sanderson, as soon as the prospect of a major dispute became clear. Burnett and the other leaders of the men warmly welcomed the Mayor's intervention, but Sanderson's initiative foundered on the bleak refusal of the Associated Employers to accept any direct negotiations with the Nine Hours League. Even at this early stage, however, uncommitted public opinion was receiving a clear impression of moderation and reason on one side and blank intransigence on the other.

Early in June one or two of the smaller engineering works gave up the struggle and conceded the fifty-four-hour week, but on both sides the major groupings remained opposed. On 6th June the League made its first issue of strike pay—three shillings each for the men who had come out prematurely on 15th May. Their impetuosity had resulted in considerable distress among them, and so their support had to be given first priority on the limited funds so far available. A week later the first general issue of strike pay was made, but this only amounted to one shilling and ninepence per man. However, by 20th June the weekly figure was up to three shillings, with sixpence for each child; by mid-August the figure was six shillings, with one shilling per child, and by October the basic weekly allowance for each worker was twelve shillings. Cowen's support was crucial, in providing an explicit guarantee for strike pay in the early part of the dispute. From the beginning the League committee managed financial affairs adroitly. Strike pay was administered in block grants to the men of the different works involved, payment being channelled through the individual delegates on the League committee, which bolstered their position. The League leaders incurred minimal expenses themselves, and regularly published meticulous accounts.

On 19th June the League organized a great rally on Newcastle Town Moor, taking pains to demonstrate the men's unity and the conspicuous orderliness and moderation of the strikers. In mid-June members of the Social Science Congress, which was then meeting in Newcastle, made another attempt at mediation. This too, however, failed, although during the attempt the League contrived to present a good, and the employers a thoroughly bad, image to uncommitted public opinion.

By the end of June the League's financial problems began to ease off somewhat. There were two main reasons for this. On the one hand the flow of donations to strike funds from sympathizers in the area and elsewhere was increasing, and on the other the numbers to be supported markedly declined, as many of the strikers succeeded in finding other employment. The Associated Employers on

Tyneside urged fellow-employers elsewhere to refuse employment to Tyneside strikers, on the grounds that the Tyneside masters were fighting the battle of employers in general, but these pleas had little effect. In the existing boom conditions for engineering works, other employers showed themselves more anxious to seize the chance to recruit valuable skilled men, rather than sacrifice their own interests for the sake of Armstrong and his associates who, as the strike continued, appeared increasingly ham-handed in the way in which they were handling the dispute. By mid-June about half of the main body of strikers had found other work, and by the time that the strike ended in October less than two thousand remained dependent on the League's funds. The revenue-raising aspect of the League's activities was not the least remarkable of that *ad hoc* body's achievements, since some £20,000 was collected and distributed during the course of the strike.

The part played in the strike by trade unions was very limited. It was not until 22nd July that the ASE headquarters came out clearly to urge branches in other parts of the country to contribute to the Tyneside strike funds, though some branches were doing so earlier on their own initiative. Some labour historians, notably the Webbs, strongly criticized the ASE for its tardy and limited intervention, but the criticism is not entirely well founded. The national leadership of the ASE were well aware of the distinct rebuff administered by the local leadership during the earlier Wearside dispute. There was, however, another important consideration. For the strike to succeed, it was crucially important that it should not alienate the public opinion to which the League appealed skilfully and successfully. Burnett and his colleagues knew how important it was for the League to maintain a good public image, and in the Britain of 1871 there was much to be said for avoiding the impression that the League was an agent of organized trade unionism. The nature of trade unionism was then under close public scrutiny, and some of the evidence of outrages at Sheffield and elsewhere, which had been widely publicized, had damaged the public reputation of trade unions. It was much more skilful to portray the Nine Hours League as simply a temporary alliance of the men to obtain one major concession for edifying purposes rather than as part of the long-term insidious pressure of organized unionism. It was of course true also that only a small minority of the men involved in the strike were members of a union. In any event, there can be no doubt that the part played by the trade unions was insignificant when compared with the local leadership of the strike.

In mid-July Charles Mark Palmer tried to use his relatively uncommitted position and his personal prestige by coming forward as a voluntary mediator. The League welcomed his intervention gratefully, while Palmer's fellow-employers gave his move a very cold reception which prevented any progress. Again the failure to achieve a settlement was generally attributed to the employers' inflexibility.

ATTEMPTS TO BREAK THE STRIKE

Early in August the employers, worried by the long duration of the strike and the men's unbroken solidarity, decided to make a move. They still flatly refused to accept the League's leaders as their workers' accredited representatives. Instead, bills were posted throughout the affected area addressed simply 'To the workmen'; these bills stated that on Thursday 3rd August the gates of the engineering works would be opened and employment offered on the basis of the fifty-seven-hour basic working week which was already the accepted system in the Clydeside engineering industry. The League leaders at once summoned a mass meeting of their followers to discuss this move, and this proposed compromise was decisively repudiated. Scarcely any men returned to the Tyneside engineering works on 3rd August, and with this failure the Associated Employers determined to go fully over to the offensive and implement contingency plans they had already been considering. In order to break the strike the masters embarked upon a major programme of recruitment of blackleg labour.

This was a move that the League had been expecting, and counter-measures were soon in hand. Burnett himself visited the London headquarters of the International Working Men's Association—the First International—with a view to using the contacts of that body to impede overseas recruiting by the employers. In fact the influence exerted by the First International in practice was very slight, but the move suggests an interesting breadth of insight by the local strike leaders.

The employers imported well over a thousand workmen from Belgium, Germany, Denmark, Norway and Sweden, at very great expense. In addition, recruiting teams were sent to other parts of Britain. At Dundee, for instance, some two hundred men were induced to sign on for work on Tyneside in return for the payment of a five shilling signing-on fee and promise of a free passage and good wages. Of the two hundred who accepted the five shillings, only about half turned up to sail, and when these men reached Tyneside the League's agents persuaded most of them to return home again at the League's expense instead of remaining in the area as acknowledged enemies of their fellow workers. The ASE leadership helped to arrange the repatriation of imported workers, and Joseph Cowen advanced money to the union to enable them to get on with this work.

With the arrival of blacklegs in force, retaliatory tactics by the local workmen and their supporters became more strenuous. There had already been some disturbances arising out of the stoppage, but these increased in number and seriousness during July and August. The local magistrates' courts had to deal with a variety of cases involving clashes between blacklegs and local folk. For example early in July one firm imported a group of workers from Sunderland to remove some completed boilers out of their works, and this led to a clash with strikers and supporters; stones were thrown, and there were a number of assaults on the Sunderland men. At Newcastle a striker was sentenced to two months' imprisonment for one of these attacks. A parallel case at Gateshead has added interest; there a lad of seventeen was given fourteen days' imprisonment for throwing stones at the Sunderland men and shouting slogans like, 'The Commune, sink the damned blacklegs'. The presiding magistrate remarked:

To imagine that persons in this country could shout for the Commune, and obstruct their neighbours with impunity, was to imagine something much too preposterous to be tolerated.

It transpired during these proceedings that the youth concerned was not an engineering worker, but merely a militant sympathizer. It cannot be seriously supposed that in expressing enthusiasm for the Paris Commune he was truly representative of the opinion of British workers. During recent months both the national and the provincial press, including the pro-strike *Newcastle Chronicle*, had been fully covering the detailed story of the Commune, and its bloody suppression amid atrocities on both sides. It would require a singularly robust act of faith to suppose that such an outbreak was more likely to help British workers than something like the studied and effective moderation of the Nine Hours League. Certainly, in the proceedings of the League there was not a trace of revolutionary political fervour, and instead there seems to have been a careful avoidance of political involvement and a deliberate concentration on the limited objective specified for the League.

Nevertheless there was sufficient disorder, and apprehended danger of more, during the summer of 1871 to present the local authorities with serious problems. Moreover, the local police had problems of their own. During 1870 and 1871 there was a series of difficulties within the Newcastle police force, caused partly by dissatisfaction over pay and working conditions, and in part by the attitude of a stern Chief Constable. The total strength of the Newcastle force was only about 160; during 1870 nearly half of this number had to be replaced, and in 1871 there was a mass resignation by eighty-seven constables. Any attempt to use the local police resources against the striking engineering workers was fraught with further difficulty, in view of the close watch maintained by Joseph Cowen and other radical members of the Newcastle Town Council. Moreover, the engineering workers were not the only group on strike at this time. Local bakers and joiners also came out in pursuit of their own objectives, and the joiners' strike in particular added its own quota to the assaults on blacklegs and similar disturbances. The Newcastle police mobilized a special flying squad of six mounted constables under Inspector Hardin, but there was too much sporadic violence around to make this an effective deterrent.

The blacklegs imported by Armstrong himself were given quarters in the Elswick works, after a little experience of the temper of the local population. On 11th August a contingent of recruits arrived from London and, after running the gauntlet of a jeering crowd on landing in the Tyne, they moved into their new billets in the Elswick works. The League responded by holding a mass meeting in the immediate vicinity of the works, and Burnett later described the scene:

Comparisons were freely instituted between Armstrong's Factory and a common lodging-house, and sarcastic remarks were made upon the violation of the factory rules, to say nothing of the excise laws, by the employers, who had large quantities of beer and tobacco taken into the factories for the use of the imprisoned knobsticks. This meeting was the severest trial of temper to which the Newcastle men were subjected, during the strike, and they came through it manfully—not the slightest disposition to molest the south countrymen being manifested . . .

The next day the *Newcastle Chronicle* added its own description of the strikers' meeting and its attitude to the blacklegs:

Many questions were asked on how they liked their imprisonment, and not a few insinuations were thrown out concerning their previous histories; but with the exception of the chaff and laughter which greeted these sallies, there was no disturbance of any kind created.

Gratifying as such evidences of restraint must have seemed to contemporary society at a time when newspapers were so often full of reports of 'trade union outrages', this was not the whole story. There were more violent activities, and the strikers and their friends very often did manifest a strong disposition to molest the imported workmen whether native or foreign. Life for a blackleg on Tyneside during the summer of 1871 was neither safe nor pleasant. Many instances could be cited, but the following is a pretty typical one, taken from the columns of the strikers' principal press supporter, the *Newcastle Chronicle*:

Yesterday evening, between six and seven o'clock, as a workman employed at Hawthorn's factory was going along Clayton Street, he was surrounded by a number of persons, who commenced hooting him, and a crowd soon gathered. He was followed some distance, and to escape further annoyance he went into a public house. Some policemen shortly afterwards came and escorted him along to the Westgate Police Station for protection from the crowd. On the way he was again hooted and a lad was taken into custody for annoying him. The man was kept in the station until the crowd was dispersed, and then he was conducted to his lodgings.

In 1871 the Liberal government legislated with the intention of defining what were and what were not permissible tactics during a strike. Questions of picketing, molestation and intimidation are, however, extremely difficult to define satisfactorily and the definitions attempted in the 1871 legislation—as in earlier and later attempts to produce legal certainty in these matters—still left ample room for conflicting interpretations. In 1871 the magistrates' courts on Tyneside had to deal with a long series of cases alleging molestation and the magistrates did not find the law very clear. Decisions varied markedly, and there was a number of acquittals, including one splendidly Gilbertian judgement delivered by B. J. Prockter, Esq, JP:

The Bench are not satisfied that there is sufficient evidence to convict the defendants, and they are dismissed. And now, my men take care and don't do it again.

This was a case in which the evidence seemed clear enough that a couple of Newcastle men had beaten up a Belgian workman.

Apart from these more serious manifestations of unfriendliness, the imported workers were the targets of a good deal of ridicule; squibs and jokes were levelled at them in the streets, in the pubs and in the local music halls.

Throughout the strike Burnett publicly and repeatedly urged his followers to abstain from any kind of violent or illegal conduct. The later recollections of a member of the police flying squad specifically mentioned Burnett's championship of peaceable methods. This policeman had been a key witness in obtaining the conviction of one of the men responsible for a particularly brutal attack on a German workman, and Burnett forbade any attempt by his supporters to retaliate against the policeman by pressure on the Watch Committee. Indeed Burnett told the policeman concerned that the verdict had been justified, and that there were others concerned who were lucky to avoid prosecution.

We need not suppose that this attitude of notable restraint proceeded from any particular regard for blacklegs, nor need we suppose that this conspicuously non-violent stance by the strike leaders had much effect in practice in hindering the operations of their more vigorous supporters. It was, however, of paramount importance to stress in every possible way the essentially responsible and respectable nature of the League's campaign, in order to appeal, and appeal successfully, to a wide spectrum of public opinion, only too likely to be alienated by a parade of violence. It is not necessary to believe that men as able and acute as Burnett and the other strike leaders were ignorant of what was going on in the streets of Tyneside towns during these months, or that they were particularly incensed by it, provided that the League's public image was not tarnished by too obtrusive violence.

VICTORY FOR THE NINE HOURS LEAGUE

It would be ingenuous indeed to accept at face value all the assurances given by Leaguers that their activities were invariably peaceful. The combination of a skilful and conspicuously non-violent leadership equipped with a large supply of emollient phrases, together with a good deal of effective intimidation in practice, was a singularly successful one. Certainly the picture of the strikers painted by the League's own propaganda was the one which overwhelmingly prevailed in contemporary opinion.

This favourable public image diminished the effectiveness of the employers' case. The Associated Employers found the cost of importing blacklegs high, at least £20,000 being spent on this activity. Believing that they were not simply fighting a local industrial dispute, but a key battle for all employers, Armstrong and his colleagues appealed for subventions from employers elsewhere:

The engineering firms who are now struck against are, in fact, fighting the battle of all employers of labour, and their yielding would be a signal for a claim for a similar reduction in the hours of labour all over the country. If the reduction of the working hours obtained, then men would no doubt continue to make other exorbitant demands, with the result of a complete disturbance of every branch of trade, and probably of a conflict between capital and labour disastrous alike to employers and employed.

There was a good deal of truth in the argument that this was more than a merely local dispute, but the appeal of the Tyneside employers for financial support proved a failure. There can be no doubt that a major reason for this was the attitude of uncommitted public opinion to the strike. Among contemporary journals of note the *Spectator* and the *Pall Mall Gazette* praised the League and supported its case. Even the employers' own professional journals, *Engineering* and *The Engineer*, did not back the Tyneside employers with any enthusiasm, and both wrote in praise of the League's skilful management. On 11th September *The Times* added its ponderous weight in an editorial which, though inaccurate in detailed information, clearly condemned the employers and praised the League. This development angered Armstrong, and he embarked upon a lengthy statement of the employers' case, which *The Times* published on 14th September. Armstrong's recourse to the press was not a great success, for a few days later *The Times* published an equally long and much more cogent letter from Burnett putting forward the men's case with a skill which added to the strike leader's increasing reputation. Demonstrations of sympathy for the League multiplied as August and September passed. On 15th September, for instance, *Engineering* reported meetings for this purpose in London, Liverpool, Manchester, Leeds, Birmingham and Sheffield. An attempt by employers on Tees-side to impede regular collections there for the League's funds collapsed under the threat of something like a local general strike.

Faced with a deteriorating position the employers resorted to the courts. On 19th September the Gateshead magistrates' court heard a batch of cases against workmen accused of offences under the Masters and Servants Acts. The bench found the defendants guilty, whereupon the prisoners expressed unanimous willingness to go to prison rather than have any fines paid, while the League reacted by arranging bail and giving notice of appeal against the verdict, which would have the effect of at least delaying proceedings until December. The Newcastle bench, hearing a similar batch of cases, came to a different conclusion, finding for the defendants, and here the employers had to give notice of appeal. All in all, the recourse to the courts did not help the employers, especially as the League used the bringing of these cases as clear evidence to discredit the claims of the employers that their imported substitutes had rendered the services of their old workers unnecessary.

After these proceedings Sir William Armstrong again resorted to the columns of *The Times*, but now his voice was distinctly muted. His second letter, published on 22nd September, spoke of misunderstandings, and hinted at arbitration as a way out. Things were not going well for the employers. They were losing valuable contracts, while the League seemed as strong as ever after four months' stoppage. Burnett at once responded to the new note in Armstrong's letter with another letter to *The Times* published on 28th September, in which he suggested that the strikers would be willing to take a wage cut in return for the concession of the fifty-four-hour week. This offer he made on his own responsibility, and there was in this instance some grumbling among his followers, though eventually the League accepted its President's initiative. In any event the offer was more impressive than realistic, for in existing boom conditions, with considerable competition for skilled labour, a wage cut was not likely to be real or lasting, while the reduction in the basic working week should be a permanent gain.

These exchanges between the principal protagonists brought about yet another attempt at mediation, this time by the Sheffield MP and industrialist, A. J. Mundella, a strong supporter of arbitration and conciliation in industrial relations. Again the League warmly welcomed his initiative, and accompanied this mediation attempt with a great demonstration on 29th September, attended by some fifteen to twenty thousand strikers and sympathizers. Even now the Associated Employers could not bring themselves to face the nasty medicine of surrender, and Mundella's efforts failed, and in announcing his failure he made no secret of his sympathy with the men's side of the case and his distaste for the employers' inflexibility.

By the end of September the Associated Employers were aware of the consequences of their long intransigence, and were fairly obviously looking for some way out which they could grasp without too much loss of face. In their public statements they now narrowed the dispute to an expression of supposed fears that if they conceded the fifty-four-hour week the engineering workers might refuse to work the overtime necessary to meet contract dates. These were hints of a virtual willingness to surrender. Early in October Joseph Cowen, and R. P. Philipson, the very influential Town Clerk of Newcastle, put their heads together and drafted a short peace formula. This proposed the introduction of the fifty-four-hour week from January 1872, no cut in wage rates, and an undertaking by the men to work overtime necessary to meet contracts. Cowen secured the assent of the League to these terms, Philipson dealt with the beaten employers, and the strike was over. With the main dispute settled, G. R. Stephenson at once extended the fifty-four-hour week to his own workers; at Palmer's works the new altered arrangements for the working week brought a short strike there, but Palmer again intervened personally with his own work force to settle matters with little trouble.

There can be no doubt where victory lay in this prolonged combat. The engineering employers of Tyneside, led by one of the most illustrious entrepreneurs of Victorian Britain, had suffered a very clear defeat at the hands of their workers. The employers had played their hand very badly indeed. In addition to their persistent refusal to talk to the men's elected leadership, Armstrong and his associates had resorted to tactics which did the strikers little harm in practice but exerted powerful effects on public opinion. There were attempts to bring pressure on shopkeepers to impede the food supply of strikers' families, strikers' children were excluded from works schools during the dispute, there was even an attempt to exclude strikers' wives from local maternity charities. On the other hand the strike leaders never put a foot wrong in their public relations. Public opinion both nationally and locally was overwhelmingly on the men's side, so that the League benefited from subscriptions and support from all levels of society and enjoyed the unequivocal support of the bulk of the influential press organs of the day.

POSTSCRIPT

After the final settlement it was obviously inexpedient for Burnett to return to his old work at Elswick, so for the next few years he worked partly for Cowen's *Chronicle* and partly for Joseph Chamberlain's Education League. He then succeeded William Allan as general secretary of the ASE. His tenure of that post was not particularly happy, however, for it was marked by repeated disagreements between Burnett and more militant sections of the union. Fortunately an alternative appeared. In 1886 the Liberal government decided to set up a Labour Bureau within the organization of the Board of Trade, an important recognition of the state's interest in industrial relations. Mundella was the minister responsible for this innovation, and had of course met Burnett during his attempted mediation in 1871. It was therefore not surprising that Burnett was chosen for this new civil service post. In 1891 the Conservative government appointed him to the Royal Commission on Labour; when in 1893 the new Liberal government embarked on a major enlargement of the labour department of the Board of Trade, Burnett remained at its head as a senior civil servant. During his later years Burnett acted on many occasions as a mediator in industrial disputes. When he died suddenly early in 1914 the event was marked by eulogistic obituaries in such establishment organs as *The Times* and the *Annual Register*. Like his friend Thomas Burt of the Northumberland miners, who became a junior minister in Liberal governments and a Privy Councillor, Burnett was something of a showpiece working man in the late Victorian establishment, living evidence of how in that society a worker could rise to positions of distinction and influence. It may be, however, that Burnett's most distinguished services to labour were those involved in his very skilful leadership of the Nine Hours Strike of 1871.

The second postscript is this. The men's victory in the 1871 strikes did not prove merely a local or a sectional one. In the wake of the surrender on Tyneside, engineering employers elsewhere were obliged to concede the fifty-four-hour week, while many other groups of workers were spurred on to seek similar concessions. In North-East England the miners' unions had been among the most generous supporters of the striking engineering workers. This was not mere altruism, for the colliery workshops employed many men in the same skilled trades and the gains won in the Tyneside engineering works could not be denied to the engineering workers employed by the local coal mines. In the weeks after the surrender of the Tyneside engineering masters, the newspapers contained many accounts of pressure for reduced working hours by other groups of men. There was more to it than that, though, for the 1871 strike was about much more than the nominal struggle about hours of work. It also involved, and was widely seen to involve, such general concepts as the employer's freedom to do as he willed with his own and on the other hand the worker's right to see to it that his own interests were considered in the way the business was managed. The men's victory in the 1871 engineers' strike marked a significant step in the capacity of organized labour to exercise effective influence in the conduct of industry.

Four

American Parallels

Strikes have not of course been a particularly British phenomenon, and the object of this chapter is to present a summary account of three American strikes. As in Britain, the history of industrial relations has been an area of American social history which has seen a tremendous growth of interest over the last quarter-century or so. Again as in Britain, attention has often been concentrated on major industrial confrontations which aroused widespread notoriety, and we should be wary of regarding these events as particularly representative of the normal course of industrial relations in America. It is also true, in America as in Britain, that the history of industrial relations is an area in which historical investigation is complicated by the subject matter's apparent relevance to present-day ideological and political matters in which social historians may be much concerned. In many modern accounts of industrial disputes in America, as in Britain, the authors have been happier in delineating the role of the workers involved, less successful in depicting the role of employers and managers, because of the possession of predisposed sympathies towards one side in an industrial conflict.

There have been some significant differences between Britain and America in the ways in which industrial relations have developed. One of these has been the rate at which trade unionism developed in the two countries. Traditions of individual responsibility and independence proved more pervasive in the younger society, and for very many years trade unions covered only a very small minority of the work force. As late as the early 1930s American trade unions could claim a total of only about four million members, and these were still very largely restricted to unions among the skilled craft workers. Even in the later 1960s only only about one in four of American workers were union members, although this generalized figure conceals a very wide disparity in unionization between different industries. In Britain, on the other hand, the Donovan Commission estimated that in 1966, out of a total work force of fourteen million manual workers and nine million white-collar workers, more than ten million workers were trade union members; half of this membership was held by nine very large unions, while four-fifths of the total belonged to less than forty unions. There were also significant differences between the ways in which American and British unions organized their affairs; in particular American unions displayed a much greater willingness among their members to support a substantial corps of full-time officials. The Donovan Commission's report included an estimate of one official to three hundred members in American unions, as against a British figure of one to three thousand.

Other differences have reflected the very different make-up of the populations concerned. The continuing flood of immigration into America for many years provided a major pool of reserve labour, much of it facing problems of integration which made effective collective action difficult. Relations between native-born American workers and immigrant groups were for many years marked by frequent friction, and of course questions of colour and race further complicated the American scene. When Britain faced problems of this order, as in the substantial Irish immigration of the nineteenth century, the difficulties involved were on a much smaller scale, though friction was not unknown during that process too. For the many years in which America was a great melting-pot of newcomers from many different origins, with much of the country exhibiting the qualities of a developing frontier society, the conduct of industrial relations, and especially of major disputes, was marked by a much higher level of violence than Britain experienced over the same period, though of course in Britain too industrial conflicts were not always conducted in a completely non-violent mode. The three disputes considered here illustrate some of the differences between the two contexts, though with some obvious similarities too.

HOMESTEAD 1892

Andrew Carnegie was born at Dunfermline in Scotland in 1835. His family emigrated to the USA in 1848, and the young Andrew Carnegie entered upon a conspicuously successful business career within the expanding American economy. By the time he was twenty-eight years old, his income had grown to an annual figure of some 50,000 dollars. When he was thirty years old, he entered the iron and steel industry. In 1883, when he had already built up a formidable multi-million dollar empire, he acquired the Homestead steel mill, east of Pittsburgh. By 1890 the Carnegie interests dominated the American iron and steel industry, with well over a quarter of the country's entire production concentrated in his plants. While Carnegie himself frequently expressed enlightened views on social questions and became one of the most prominent philanthropists of his day, the history of industrial relations within the Carnegie empire was far from smooth and there was frequent hostility between management and workers. Trade unionism was vulnerable partly because of the continual supply of immigrant labour, and because of the racial and cultural differences which existed within the work force. In addition the small trade unions established among the skilled men maintained extremely exclusive policies, denying membership not only to labourers but also to the developing categories of semi-skilled workers. Exclusiveness also existed in the conventions whereby certain groups of key skilled men had become dominated by distinctive groups, such as Irish or Welsh immigrants. Strikes in Carnegie plants in the 1880s had been bitterly fought and marked by considerable outbreaks of violence. In general these conflicts saw a series of successes for the Carnegie management in cutting the influence of the skilled trade unions. In 1890 a three months' strike in the Carnegie coke works was marked by sabotage, arson and a high level of violence; the strike ended in a clear-cut victory for the management.

In 1889 a new three-year wage agreement had been introduced for the Homestead plant, and this was due to end in the summer of 1892. Before this period ended, the management had determined to use the expiry date as the occasion for a showdown with the Amalgamated Association of Iron and Steel Workers, the union of a small minority of skilled workers performing key functions in the plant. In the past this union had exercised considerable influence in iron and steel works by exploiting the key functions in the production processes carried out by its members. Its members were very much an aristocracy of labour, insisting on good pay and conditions for themselves, but maintaining a strong exclusive barrier against other groups of workers.

During the early months of 1892 the Carnegie managers, effectively led by Henry Clay Frick, prepared for trouble. In January the management made known its terms for a new pay agreement; these terms involved cuts in many rates of payment, and changes in established negotiating procedures obviously intended to operate in the management's interests. The company was determined to have its way and had no intention of receding from this ultimatum. It was some time before the Amaglamated Association woke up to the seriousness of the challenge being posed to its influence; a last-minute recruiting campaign brought in a few hundred new members from the Homestead plant, but the main union involved was still the organization of a small and exclusive minority of the workers employed in the plant.

Early in May Carnegie himself sailed for Europe, and for the greater part of the conflict which followed he was comfortably insulated by distance from immediate responsibility for the conduct of the bitter dispute. In June the company began direct preparations in advance of the expiry on 24th June of the existing wage agreement and the firm's ultimatum. A metal fence, twelve feet high, was erected all round the land approaches to the Homestead plant. On 20th June Frick wrote to the Pinkerton detective agency warning them that a dispute impended and that the company would want to hire large numbers of guards; Pinkertons already had considerable experience in the provision of men for industrial espionage, strike-breaking, and guarding premises during industrial disputes.

It was not until late in the same month that the Amalgamated Association formed a committee to handle the workers' side of the dispute. At the Homestead works the management brought about peak production in the weeks running up to the final crisis. Then on 28th June, without warning, the firm closed down some departments of the works, laying off some eight hundred men. Mass meetings of the other workers, the overwhelming majority of whom were not union members, agreed to strike. Anticipating that the company might try to bring in blacklegs or strike-breaking guards, the men's leaders organized very strong picketing forces; these included a total of some four thousand men, together with a flotilla of boats to watch traffic on the river Monongahela, which was one of the main routes in and out of the works. By 2nd July the whole of the great Homestead works lay idle, while the company made no secret of the fact that it had no intention of ever recognizing a trade union in the plant again; in future the firm would regard and deal with all workers simply as individuals.

One reason for the frequency of violence on such occasions was the relative weakness of the formal agencies of local government in industrial settlements such as this area of Pennsylvania. The major firms had in practice dominated the local scene. Certainly in the townships inhabited by the Homestead workers, the local law enforcement agencies were incapable of mobilizing forces sufficient to dominate the scene, and in circumstances of a mass strike such as this it was quite impossible to raise sufficient volunteer supporters to remedy the paucity of local police resources. In the townships themselves effective local control passed to the workers' strike organization.

Meanwhile, on Frick's instruction Pinkertons collected more than three hundred men to act as 'guards' for the Homestead plant. These men were a very motley crew, mostly recruited in New York and Chicago. They were brought into Pennsylvania by train, together with supplies of firearms and ammunition. Near Pittsburgh the small army was transferred into two river barges belonging to the Carnegie company, which had been converted for this troop-carrying role. On 5th July the little squadron was towed along the river towards the Homestead plant, with the objective of having the men enter the works under cover of darkness. However, as the barges were towed along the last stretch of their journey, they were spotted by pickets, and sporadic shooting broke out. At dawn on 6th July the barges grounded on the shore beside the Homestead works, where a huge array of strikers had gathered, many of them armed. When the Pinkerton recruits tried to go ashore, heavy firing resulted, with considerable bloodshed on both sides. The would-be Homestead guards were effectively pinned down on their barges, their assailants employing pistols, rifles, dynamite and even a couple of old and decrepit cannon. The Pinkerton men were in a very dangerous position and, as the summer day wore on, in increasing discomfort, especially their wounded. Finally negotiations took place, which resulted in an agreement by the Pinkerton men that they would surrender themselves and their weapons in return for safe conduct out of the area. It was with very great difficulty that the strike leaders managed to see that these terms were reasonably well carried out, and that no massacre of the prisoners ensued. There were in fact a fair number of assaults on the vanquished party, but they were finally extricated from the area. The barges in which they had landed were triumphantly burned by the victorious strikers. the death toll of the fighting was probably nine strikers and seven Pinkerton men, with very many others wounded in varying degree.

Elsewhere there were some expressions of sympathy for the strikers, though nothing which involved very significant aid in the struggle. Carnegie had given Keir Hardie £100 towards his expenses in the British general election of 1892, and Hardie now gave this money to Homestead strike funds.

Another kind of purported help proved to be of much more harm than assistance to the strikers' cause. In Worcester, Massachusetts, two recent immigrants were living together, Alexander Berkman and Emma Goldman; both were of Russian Jewish origin and shared militant left-wing political beliefs. Berkman, who came from a middle-class social background in Vilna, decided that if he assassinated Frick, the current personification of the capitalist oppressors, it would not only encourage the Carnegie strikers but would encourage workers everywhere to join in revolutionary activities. He accordingly embarked first on certain experiments in bomb-making, but his technical knowledge and equipment proved sadly inadequate. He subsequently, with some difficulty, raised enough money to buy a pistol and to make his way to the scene of the dispute.

Meanwhile, at Homestead another development had greatly reduced the strikers' ability to command the situation. The Carnegie company and the local authorities had from the beginning of the dispute put pressure on the Governor of Pennsylvania to bring in National Guard units to take control of the situation and ensure the maintenance of law and order. Governor Pattison had shown reluctance to take this action, though it was by no means uncommon for the Pennsylvania National Guard to be mobilized and sent into action in the course of industrial disputes. After a series of formal requests by local law enforcement agencies Pattison decided that he must act, and accordingly in late July powerful units of the National Guard moved into the Homestead area under a commanding officer who soon showed himself hostile to the strikers. With the arrival of the state troopers it became increasingly difficult for the strikers to prevent the firm from introducing blacklegs into the works; there was a certain amount of friction between troopers and the local inhabitants, but the presence of large bodies of armed soldiers transformed the situation. There were one or two instances of sympathy for the strike by members of the National Guard, but these were firmly quashed. After the arrival of the troops, steps were taken for the prosecution of the strike leaders involved in the battle of 6th July.

By this time Alexander Berkman had made his way to the scene of the dispute. Posing as an agent who could obtain blackleg workers, he easily obtained access to Frick's headquarters. On 23 July he attacked Frick, shooting him twice in the neck and then stabbing him with a sharpened file during a struggle. Berkman was seized, and the wounded Frick insisted during the fracas, 'Don't shoot, leave him to the law'. Frick's injuries were not very serious, and he was only confined to bed for ten days. During the period of his recovery his month-old baby child died. Berkman's ideas of the likely result of his intervention were wildly misconceived, for his victim, who continued to direct the company's affairs from his sick-bed, became a hero, and Berkman himself the subject of execration. Even the strikers could scarcely miss the point that this violence had gravely hampered their cause in the eyes of uncommitted public opinion; and there can be no doubt that Berkman's action did the strikers much more harm than good, and there was not the slightest sign of the revolutionary snowball on which Berkman had counted. At Berkman's trial he was given a total of twenty-one years' imprisonment, by prosecuting him on multiple charges and awarding consecutive maximum sentences.

The strike continued into August, but public interest in it rapidly waned elsewhere in the country. New news items came along—the Lizzie Borden case broke early in August, the Dalton brothers were killed early in October. The strikers remained doggedly out for week after week, but the presence of the National Guard made it possible for the company to move increasing numbers of blacklegs into the Homestead works. Even so, production remained negligible. Sporadic punch-ups involving blacklegs continued, but by late September the strike unmistakably faced failure, with the company flatly refusing to enter into any negotiations with union representatives.

At the end of September there was an unexpected and unprecedented legal intervention. Paxson, Chief Justice of Pennsylvania, laid it down that the leaders of the strike involved in the 6th July battle were guilty of treason to the state of Pennsylvania. This judgement was subsequently to be the target of harsh criticism by expert legal authorities, but at the time it played a part in ensuring the strike's failure by putting behind bars some of its main leaders. By mid-October there was already a trickle of skilled steel workers back to the Homestead plant on the company's terms, and by the middle of the month the last of the National Guard units was withdrawn from the scene. By the end of October almost all of Carnegie's iron and steel empire was back in full production. In mid-November, after a heroic and lengthy struggle with very meagre resources, the day labourers and mechanics involved in the strike had to ask the Amalgamated Association to release them from the pledges of solidarity they had made when the strike began, and on 20th November, by a narrow majority, the remaining strikers agreed to abandon the struggle. At its height the strike had involved some thirteen thousand men, including some sympathetic strikers from other Carnegie plants. Of the four thousand or so Homestead workers the company only re-engaged about one third, and some strike leaders were blacklisted for life throughout the iron and steel industry. Union influence at Homestead and in other Carnegie plants was broken, and it was not until the First World War that wages again reached the figure of early 1892. Alexander Berkman was released from prison in 1919 and deported from America; in poverty and sickness, he shot himself in Paris.

US STEEL 1919

Major strikes took place in the American iron and steel industry during the early twentieth century. Like the Carnegie strike already described, some of these involved serious violence and bloodshed. Two instances of this kind were the strike of January 1916 at Republic Steel's Ohio installations and the subsequent dispute in

April of the same year in the United States Steel plant at Braddock, Pennsylvania.

Pressures involved in the First World War increased some areas of likely conflict. The war was marked by a significant increase in the Federal government's intervention in industrial affairs, with influence being exerted to maintain production for the war effort, even if this meant an increased recognition of the functions of trade unionism, and pressure on employers to make concessions to avoid disputes. Labour shortages and the need to maintain wartime production induced employers in the industry to accept welfare schemes and conciliatory attitudes which did not persist unchecked into the following years of peace. By 1919 there was widespread determination among management in iron and steel to make it plain that the prerogatives of management should be sustained. There was in particular a determination to ensure that management should not be coerced by trade unions in matters of how plants should be organized and operated. At the same time many companies created and supported 'company unions', that is labour organizations in which their own work force was grouped in associations limited to the enterprise concerned and usually subject to considerable company influence. These institutions were normally linked with a determination to outlaw pressures from 'outside' organizations, such as the ordinary industrial trade unions. At the same time in many cases the activities of these 'company unions' were linked with welfare schemes of varying degrees of coverage and scale.

On the labour side the concessions won under the extraordinary circumstances of wartime had whetted the appetite for more, and when peace came the union leadership found themselves faced with considerable militancy among their followers. This was the case despite the moderate level of trade union membership which had been attained, and the persistence of serious divisions between different groups of workers, notably the skilled/unskilled and native born/immigrant relationships which were continuously sensitive and often coincided as sources of friction.

With the end of the war came a continuing rise in the cost of living and the reduction of some of the wartime opportunities for overtime. In the summer of 1919 union officials in the iron and steel industry—though not only there—found themselves under increasing grass-roots pressure for militant action to conserve or improve standards of living. By this time the various unions involved in this industry had come together in a rather frail national committee. In May 1919, despite well-founded doubts as to the chances of success on the part of many leading officials, that committee was forced to adopt a programme which demanded full collective bargaining rights for trade unions, no discrimination of any kind against union membership, an eight-hour day with a six-day week, an increase in wages 'sufficient to guarantee an American standard of living', standard wage scales for similar types of work, double pay for overtime, Sundays and holiday period work, collection of trade union dues by companies and the abolition of 'company unions'. In addition there was a demand for the adoption whenever lay-offs might be necessary of the 'last in, first out principle', and a specific demand for the abolition of twenty-four-hour shifts in plants working on the continuous operation principle. After this programme had been reluctantly swallowed by the national union representative committee, a national ballot of union members produced an overwhelming majority for the use of strike action if the demands were refused.

During the war the US Federal government had repeatedly intervened in industrial relations and had often forced employers to accept workers' demands in order to maintain production. There was no secret of the fact that President Wilson disliked intransigent employers and believed in the maintenance of sweet reasonableness in industrial relations. It soon transpired that the summer of 1919 was different from the recent halcyon days. United States Steel was the big corporation which became the main target of the workers' movement, and there the management were ready for a fight. Its chief executive, E. H. Gary, simply refused to enter into any negotiations with the unions, denying them any right to act as representatives of the workers employed by US Steel. The union leaders hoped that such recalcitrance could be broken by the intervention of the Federal government, as had happened frequently during the war. Here, however, circumstances worked against the unions. In the summer of 1919 Wilson was chiefly concerned with international affairs, and the timing of the strike's outbreak proved unfortunate. The union leaders met in conference on 9th–10th September and during these discussions 22nd September was fixed as the date for strike action if the unions' demands were not met. On the next day, 11th September, a presidential statement was released in which Wilson urged a three weeks' breathing space to allow time for conciliation. This mischance of timing faced union leaders with a difficult decision. To go back on the strike date fixed was to court trouble with militant followers and perhaps blunt the strike weapon, but to stick to the decision involved irritation to the President and an adverse effect on uncommitted public opinion. With great misgivings the union leaders decided to stick to their decision.

Neither side had any clear idea of the likely response to the strike call, which in the event was much more extensive than unions or management had anticipated. Something like half of the industry's entire work force came out on 22nd September; this amounted to about a quarter of a million men. Of these only about half were actually enrolled members of trade unions, despite the considerable gains in union membership registered during the war.

One of the reasons why President Wilson had pleaded for delay was a more general initiative in industrial relations. A national Industrial Conference was scheduled to meet in Washington on 6th October. This project had emanated from widely-expressed hopes that in some way the nature of post-war industrial relations could be made smoother and more amicable. The conference was to consist of three groups of delegates—workers' representatives appointed by the American Federation of Labor, leading representatives of management and a group of 'public' delegates appointed by government. By the time the conference assembled the strike in the steel industry was well under way, and this meant that the credibility of the attempt at national conciliation came to centre round discussion with a direct or indirect relationship to this major dispute. The rules adopted for the conference stipulated that all three groups must concur for any decision to be ratified. The issue of union recognition was a major point in the steel strike, and dominated the conference. Tied in with this was the question of the closed shop. Many of the 'public' delegates were anxious about the coercion of men to join unions, while the labour representatives were determined that company unions must go. By 21st October the conference was deadlocked on these issues, and the American Federation of Labor made public its decision to give full backing to the steel strike. A further complication lay in the fact that President Wilson's health had broken down; he had suffered a major stroke on 2nd October, but from his sickbed he issued an appeal to the conference to break the deadlock. Despite this, on 22nd October the national industrial conference formally failed to agree on the key issues involved. The worker and 'public' delegations were willing to adopt a modified formula defining acceptable workers' organizations and their role, but by a majority of ten to seven the employers' representatives refused to agree, because of a continued determination to resist dictation from what they regarded as 'outside' agencies, and a refusal to accept the end of company unions. The narrowness of the majority is some indication that there were divided opinions among employers. Even Gary of United Steel would have been willing to accept trade unions as negotiating bodies for their own members, provided the unions would accept individual freedom to opt out of union membership, and accept also that other bodies, including company unions, could negotiate on behalf of other groups of workers.

It was plain by the time that the conference failed to agree upon these issues that the steel strikers faced hostility from the mass of uncommitted public opinion. America faced a wide crop of strikes during these months—one out of every five workers was involved in some kind of strike action during 1919—and there was wide resentment at the inconvenience and dislocation involved. A high proportion of the steel strikers were immigrant workers, not the most popular group among older sectors of the population. The press seized upon any hint of violence, and there was a great deal of talk about the involvement of subversive political groups in the strike. Some of the strike leaders did have past associations with extremist political groups. W. Z. Foster, the secretary of the national committee of iron and steel trade unions, provided the most glaring example of such a past, and his extremist connections were raised in Congress and much discussed in the press. When Foster appeared before a Senate committee he made a poor impression and certainly failed to eradicate suspicion. Associations like this damaged the strike and greatly reduced the possibilty of official intervention on the side of the strikers. Instead, from the beginning of the strike, there were repeated examples of state forces acting against the strikers. Local authorities banned or dispersed strike rallies. In one county which was a centre of the dispute five thousand men were deputized by the county sheriff, most of those involved being organized by the strike-bound companies. There were many arrests of local leaders, some of them of very dubious legality. Again, however, there was no uniformity in the official reaction. The Mayor of Cleveland took action to prevent the entry of blacklegs into that city, until forced to desist by positive court orders obtained by employers. The Governor of Pennsylvania was, however, hostile to the strike and repeatedly refused to entertain protests against abuse of power by state authorities in that key area.

At first morale among the strikers was high. After the American Federation of Labor backed the strike, that organization raised more than 400,000 dollars for the strike funds, mainly in donations from other unions. However, this level of support could not be long continued. The affected companies embarked on plans to subvert the strike, not only by the use of blacklegs, but by such methods as the employment of undercover agents to spread defeatism among workers. The press frequently exaggerated reports of men returning to work, and made much of outrages, such as an incident in which shots were fired at a plant superintendent in Colorado. By the end of October, with conciliation unlikely, the employers began to import blacklegs in large numbers; much was made of the use of Negro labour which, while it could certainly stiffen resentment among the strikers, could also raise the spectre of permanently lost jobs. The fragility of the united front of steel workers provided a serious danger. One of the long-established unions involved, the Amalgamated Association of Iron, Steel and Tin Workers, was a union of specialized skilled men which had tenaciously fought to maintain craft privileges and had exploited the key roles of its members to extort favourable contracts of employment, while at the same time operating a policy of determined exclusion against other groups of workers. At the end of November the contracts of Association members were threatened with permanent cancellation by employers and at this threat the Association crumbled. The Association ordered its members back to work and even took disciplinary action against branches which tried to resist this instruction. The Association had withdrawn from the strike by 14th December. Nor was the absence of a united front confined to the steel industry itself. Coal miners and railwaymen might have helped to give the strike real teeth if they had taken effective action to black the strike-bound companies, but attempts to obtain such action proved ineffective.

By the end of 1919 only a minority of the original strikers were still out, and the unions surrendered on 8th January 1920, ordering the remainder of the strikers to go back to work if they could obtain their jobs back. In fact there seems to have been little in the way of blacklisting, but the end of the strike marked an unmistakably clear defeat for the unions. The action of the Amalgamated Association in leaving the strike in December was a fatal blow at the fragile national unity of labour organizations in steel, and the national committee came to an end in July 1920. W. Z. Foster emerged subsequently as a leading figure in American communism. In 1929 membership in trade unions in the steel industry was still at the level reached by 1914. Government intervention did, however, bring about some improvement in working conditions in the industry after the strike was over, notably the establishment of a standard eight-hour day. However, the story of the next strike to be considered was to be a distinctly different one.

GENERAL MOTORS 1936–7

The third American strike to be considered is the General Motors strike of the 1936–7 winter. General Motors was one of the giants of the American automobile industry, the producer of Chevrolets, Buicks, Pontiacs, Oldsmobiles, Cadillacs. Founded in 1908, the company had a varied history but after 1932 it had entered upon a period of prosperity. Like many other American companies GM had consistently opposed recognition of trade unions as negotiating agents for its work force, and had encouraged instead the growth of a company-based union with strong employer influence in its proceedings. At the same time the company had embarked upon an extensive series of paternalistic welfare schemes, providing for savings, house purchase and extensive facilities for recreation and sport. To some extent the company had responded here to prodding from Roosevelt's New Deal administration, but there had been a good deal of company initiative too. The management of General Motors, like much of America's big business world, was hostile to the Democratic administration and its policies. In industrial matters GM management was adamant that the organization and methods of production were management preserves, and the attempts of trade unions to organize GM workers were met with a variety of counter-measures. Like some other big American companies, GM was a regular customer of detective agencies like Pinkertons which were willing to supply agents for espionage and subversion in union ranks.

At the same time the nature of the industry provided a wide variety of ready-made situations capable of causing friction in industrial relations. Assembly line techniques and the use of timed working operations were undergoing constant refinement, but there were serious flaws in the methodology employed. For example, the selection of a timing for an operation which matched the abilities of an 'average' worker was unlikely to prove an adequate working context for everyone. Until the mid-1930s, however, organized trade unionism in the car industry, as in other sectors, remained weak. The central American Federation of Labor was dominated by restrictive craft unions, and even when unions in the car industry were willing to widen the base of their support by enrolling less skilled workers, the AFL adopted a very discouraging attitude. Dislike of these conservative attitudes towards unionism in the burgeoning car industry formed part of a much wider crisis blowing up inside the AFL, which was to culminate in November 1935 in the establishment of the Committee for Industrial Organization (CIO) as a major breakaway from the AFL. The United Automobile Workers had been increasingly restive under the restrictions imposed upon it by the AFL, as the price for AFL support, and its discontent with the attempts of the AFL to maintain control over the automobile union led the latter into the ranks of the fledgling CIO a little while before the major strike involved here. John L. Lewis, the leader of the CIO, knew very well that the fate of his infant organization was in great measure bound up with the outcome of the major strike in which the United Automobile Workers became involved in late 1936.

The town of Flint, Michigan, was the centre of the dispute. Here there were few of the ethnic problems which had hampered labour unity in earlier disputes; indeed, by the mid-1930s this factor, though certainly not dead, was less pervasive than it had been earlier, for many of the earlier immigrant groups were by now more settled members of the American community. Although there was more variety in other parts of the Michigan car industry, at Flint itself native-born white Americans were very predominant. The town of Flint was very much a 'company town', economically dependent on General Motors; the firm dominated local society and exercised a major influence in the not very sophisticated agencies of official local government.

The major dispute at the turn of the year was presaged by a number of partial and short-lived strikes earlier in 1936. Some of these were sit-down strikes, involving occupation of workshops by the workers, a technique by no means new but enjoying a revival in the mid-1930s in other countries as well as America. The car workers' union and the CIO were well aware that trouble was brewing in the car industry and already anticipated some major conflict, probably in the course of 1937. However, the outbreak of a major strike at the General Motors complex at Flint took them by surprise. This was scarcely surprising since the original incident was, as far as can be seen, completely spontaneous, though indicative of a pre-existing atmosphere of friction. In a General Motors plant at Cleveland, Ohio, a minor grievance emerging on 28th December 1936 sparked off a sit-down strike. On 30th December fifty out of the thousand men employed at one of the main GM plants at Flint also began a sit-down strike sparked off by a purely local grievance. By the evening of 30th December, however, this small spark had resulted in the strike spreading to a much bigger GM plant within the Flint complex of works. By 20th January the movement had snowballed, with 38,000 men involved in Flint alone, and in all something like 136,000 men became involved at one time or another throughout the GM empire. After 30th December Flint was very much the centre of the strike. The strikers built up a complex organization providing for the feeding of the men occupying factory buildings, for a variety of duties such as the picketing, for entertainment and for the maintenance of discipline. This was only one element in what rapidly emerged as a very complex dispute. CIO and car workers' unions were much involved, as of course were employers and management. Also affected were town, state and Federal government agencies. In this strike too there were frequent accusations of communist inspiration behind the dispute. That communists were present and sought to exploit the situation for their own ends is clear enough, but it is equally clear that they played neither a dominant nor a crucial role, and that they would have been impotent and insignificant had it not been for the genuine grievances arising from working conditions. This was not a political strike.

The atmosphere in which the dispute occurred was one which provided favourable circumstances for the car workers in some ways. Although the local town government was very much company-orientated, the same was not true of Michigan State or US Federal administrations. Roosevelt's New Deal administration was not hostile to trade unions or worker aspirations, while at state level a key change came on 1st January 1937 when Frank Murphy took office as Governor of Michigan. He was to exercise a crucial moderating influence, and act as one of the most important personalities involved. Another factor was that the families of strikers regularly obtained assistance from Michigan state relief agencies, which eased the financial problems of the strike. The press gave massive coverage to the strike, and was not especially hostile; a good deal of sympathetic publicity was aroused by the activities of the women's auxiliary organization which looked after many of the strikers' feeding arrangements and similar activities. In general the union's public relations were much more successful than had often been the case in earlier disputes. For example, when on 5th January a local judge issued a court injunction against the sitting-in workers, his move was essentially rendered counter-productive when the strikers publicized the fact that the judge was a General Motors shareholder.

From the beginning of the strike there ensued a complex and often secret sequence of negotiations. Behind the scenes the personal prestige of the US President was much employed, while his Secretary of Labor Frances Perkins and Governor Murphy played much more obvious roles. The course of the negotiations fluctuated with events. A seriously mishandled attempt by local police forces to evict strikers on 11th January—which has gone down in American labour history as the Battle of the Running Bulls—ended in clear victory for the strikers, and further support for them from uncommitted public opinion. Church leaders, civil liberties campaigners and similar groups strenuously criticized the company for this escapade. The methods of the company often seemed maladroit; their repeated recourse to the courts was ill-managed, for instead of limiting their legal efforts to try to win back possession of their occupied plants, they sought to obtain prohibitions against picketing, not a very popular course to take.

General Motors for long resolutely refused to accept the idea of the United Automobile Workers (UAW) as the sole recognized negotiating body for the bulk of the GM work force, and as the trail of negotiations twisted and turned time and time again, it was on this point that settlement seemed impossible. At one point when the chances of settlement seemed especially remote, on 1st February, the strikers carried out a sudden coup by occupying the plant at Flint which was the only source of engines for Chevrolet cars. This episode followed prolonged efforts by the US Secretary of Labor to bring the two sides together. Governor Murphy exercised a key moderating role throughout; he refused to allow state officers to enforce court warrants against strike leaders obtained by the Flint town authorities, who were themselves powerless against the organized strikers. For as long as possible Murphy turned a deaf ear to the repeated requests of the local authorities for the despatch of National Guard units to the Flint area. When on 13th January he did move National Guard units in to reinforce a state police presence established earlier, he passed over the most obvious officer to place in command in favour of a man more likely to exercise a moderating and conciliatory line. Murphy made it quite plain that state agencies would not be agencies of the company-dominated local government of Flint. It was Governor Murphy who first succeeded in bringing the recalcitrant GM management into actual contact with union leaders on 14th January, and under Murphy's pressure it appeared that agreement had been reached early the next day. However, disputes as to the implementation of terms prolonged the conflict. There then followed further negotiations in Washington, which dragged on till the strikers' coup on 1st February at Flint. These events brought a further crisis. Governor Murphy was in danger of being forced out of his mediating position when on 2nd February General Motors obtained a court order for the ending of the factory occupation with a deadline for the following afternoon. Unless some settlement could be reached, the state governor could not long delay the enforcement of a plain and unequivocal judicial order by a competent court. The governor finally succeeded in bringing the two sides together again, a feat which involved obtaining a personal request from Roosevelt for the company to participate. Throughout these days the President's influence was much invoked, but it was Murphy's patient and good-tempered diplomacy which played a major role in reaching a settlement on 11th February. This agreement was rather an armistice; by it the company conceded recognition of the UAW as a negotiating body for its men, and recognized that the union had a legitimate claim to a say in such matters as rates of work. The 11th February agreement was intended to lead to a much more permanent agreement, which was reached on 12th March. By this, UAW became the effective negotiating body for all GM plants, and a complex system of arrangements for the hearing and redress of workers' grievances was agreed. The union agreed to forbid stoppages of work until the resources of this machinery had been exhausted.

One major result of the 1936 dispute was a considerable boost to union membership in the car industry. UAW strength rose from 88,000 in early 1936 to around 400,000 by October 1937. By that time Chrysler and other major car producers had been forced to accept similar terms in the wake of the GM surrender. The impact of the 1936–7 strike at Flint was not, however, confined to a single industry, but formed part of a wider pattern of events affecting industrial relations in America. Apart from union activities this included a greater degree of governmental involvement. The Wagner Act of 1935, for example, had stipulated that a company must be prepared to negotiate with a union which could show that it possessed the backing of a majority of the relevant work force. During the 1936–7 strike, the La Follette congressional committee had uncovered much evidence of company malpractices including the use of anti-union espionage agents; this evidence had received widespread publicity, and included a number of examples drawn from GM's own tactics during the 1936–7 dispute.

In addition there was some evidence of an important change of heart among some at least of the key leaders of American industry. For example, Myron Taylor, an influential chief officer of the giant US Steel corporation, was by 1937 publicly urging managers to realize that co-operation with trade unions and a recognition of their legitimate aspirations was a more sensible and productive policy than continuing conflict. In the USA of the 1930s the political atmosphere was much more favourable to the development of trade unionism than it had ever been before, something for which the depression and its political repercussions were largely responsible. The GM strike and the very considerable interest which it aroused played a part in the evolution of this changed situation.

Five

The General Strike of 1926

Between the engineering strikes of 1871 and the outbreak of the First World War the position of organized labour in Britain had changed dramatically. Membership of trade unions had grown considerably, and with a total membership of well over four million in 1914 the unions now constituted a substantial minority of all British workers. In addition to this numerical growth the status of the union movement had also changed markedly. The Trades Disputes Act of 1906 had conferred extraordinary legal privileges on the unions, while the expansion of public provision in such areas as unemployment and health insurance had involved increasing links between official agencies and the accredited representatives of the workers. In the case of John Burnett we have already glimpsed something of the government's extending interest in industrial relations, and an early example of an individual moving from trade union office to an important civil service post. Such transfers had become much more common by 1914, and demonstrated one aspect of the transition by which the trade union movement was by then a respectably established element in British society.

The increase in union membership, and the movement's role in society, were both enhanced by the experience of the First World War, with the need to organize the national economy for war purposes, and the government's need to enlist trade union help in this task. By 1918 the trade unions possessed six-and-a-half million members, and the overwhelming majority of these, over five-and-a-quarter million, were affiliated to the Trades Union Congress; in the first two post-war years union membership continued its rapid growth. By 1918 also trade union leaders were accustomed to frequent contacts with government, while a few representatives of organized labour had reached ministerial and even cabinet rank in the war-time coalition governments. From the general election at the end of 1918 the Labour Party emerged with fifty-nine MPs, almost all of them sponsored and supported by trade unions.

Even before the war there had been a series of attempts to improve the level of co-operation and mutual support among the unions. Shortly before the First World War opened, a potentially powerful grouping had been reached by an agreement between three of the largest and strongest unions—the Miners' Federation of Great Britain, the National Union of Railwaymen and the National Transport Workers' Federation. This coalition was given the nickname of the 'Triple Alliance', an ironical parallel with the great power politics of Europe. The coming of war forestalled any testing of this coalition, but when the immediately post-war years ushered in a period of industrial unrest, new attempts were set on foot to re-establish a basis for this kind of mutual support between key unions.

In these years the coal industry was at the centre of industrial conflict. The mines employed about a million workers, and coal was of vital importance to the national economy. During the war the government had taken control of the mines as an emergency measure, and this temporary public control still existed in 1919, when the miners' union presented a claim for increased wages and reduced hours of working. Lloyd George had been confirmed in power by the general election late in 1918, and in 1919 he showed, at least from a short-term point of view, considerable skill in coping with the miners' demands. He induced the miners' leaders to postpone an immediate confrontation by offering a Royal Commission to examine the state of the coal industry. This expedient sufficed to stave off the possibility of 'Triple Alliance' action for the time being. When the Sankey Commission reported, later in 1919, it recommended an increase in wages and a reduction in hours; by a very narrow majority the Commission also endorsed the miners' case for the nationalization of the mines. The government responded to the Commission's recommendations on wages and hours, imposing by statute a maximum seven-hour day for face workers in the collieries. The demand for nationalization was first evaded and then when the situation seemed more favourable rejected.

In 1920 the miners faced the government, still in control of the mines, with another wage demand. When this was refused, the miners voted to take strike action in the late summer, and again appealed for support from the railwaymen and transport workers, who could impose an effective embargo on the use of alternative supplies of fuel. The government had shown a disposition to stand firm against the miners' demands, but when in October a special conference of the National Union of Railwaymen agreed to take effective action in support of the miners, the government backed down and conceded them a substantial wage increase. Faced with a potentially critical situation, including low coal stocks and no effective emergency arrangements available, the government had been forced to give in, but this coercion of the established government by elements of organized labour provided an unmistakable lesson to the political world. The Lloyd George Government in 1920 placed on the statute book the Emergency Powers Act, a measure which made available sweeping powers to a government faced with a national emergency which could not be met by the normal agencies of administration. The Act owed much to the emergency legislation enacted under the pressure of war from 1914 onwards, and under its provisions the government was in a strong position to exercise effective control of affairs in an emergency; it could, for example, requisition goods and services and impose stringent public order controls.

The 1920 wages agreement for the mines was due to end at the last day of March 1921, and before this potential crisis point arrived the government decided to rid itself of the immediate responsibility by restoring the mines to their owners. The employers made it clear that they intended to impose wage reductions. The miners were determined to resist and again turned to their allies in the railway and transport unions. The 'Triple Alliance' again seemed to work, with the miners' associates agreeing to enforce an embargo on the movement of coal from 12th April unless the threat to the miners' standard of living was withdrawn. At the same time the other unions involved pressed the miners to continue negotiations in the hope of avoiding a major conflict. The miners' tactics in handling their allies were defective, for they insisted that these supporters had no right to take part in the negotiations unless and until they were actually engaged in industrial action. This aroused understandable irritation among the leaders of the other two great unions involved. The mine owners were determined to replace the existing national conventions for wage bargaining with district agreements which would take account of the marked variations in profitability on the coalfields, and it was plain that a reversion to district agreements would involve substantial wage cuts for many miners. The government for its part would do no more than offer a strictly temporary subsidy to prolong the difficult period of transition in wage rates. There was no chance of the miners accepting this.

With some misgivings the leaders of the railwaymen and the transport workers agreed on 13th April that they would take strike action in support of the miners' resistance from the evening of Friday 15th April, and the appropriate notices for this were sent out to branches. Then on Thursday 14th April, at a meeting at the House of Commons, Frank Hodges, the secretary of the Miners' Federation, made remarks which were interpreted as suggesting that the miners might not after all be totally opposed to any form of district agreements. This was prominently reported in the newspapers the following morning, to the astonishment of the leaders of the other unions involved, who were under the impression that this was one matter on which the miners were adamant. Again the miners' leaders were distinctly tactless in their relations with their allies, and again the leaders of the other unions were distinctly irritated at the cavalier treatment they received in their understandable enquiries for information and clarification. The leaders of the railwaymen and the transport workers had been prepared to hazard the interests and the funds of their members in support of the miners, but they now found themselves faced both with inconsiderate treatment and evidence that the miners' leadership was itself divided as to how to react to their secretary's maladroit intervention. Enmeshed in a difficult and confused situation, at a heated meeting on 15th April the executives of the railwaymen and the transport workers decided overwhelmingly to call off their planned strike action in support of the miners, an event notorious in trade union history as Black Friday. The miners grimly came out in isolation and remained on strike till the beginning of July, when they were forced to return on the owners' terms of district wage agreements and, in many cases, lower rates of payment. The 1921 stoppage had in addition the effect of eroding any savings which mining families might have accumulated in previous years and made them less able to face future stoppages with reserves in hand.

BACKGROUND TO THE GENERAL STRIKE

The next few years saw a continuation, or rather a worsening, of the basic problems facing the British coal industry, though these were in some degree masked by the temporary intervention of external events, something which had in fact already happened in 1921, when a prolonged coal strike in America had given a short-lived fillip to British sales. It is often said that the British coal industry was antiquated and inefficient, but this is something of an over-generalization. It is true that the organization of the mines left much to be desired, with some 1,400 individual enterprises operating about 2,500 collieries, while in some other great industries amalgamations and consolidations had effected a more efficient operating pattern in previous years. In reality the situation of the British coal industry was very far from uniform. There was very considerable variation in the position of different coalfields. In some areas, such as Nottinghamshire and South Yorkshire, recent development had created important areas of new and profitable collieries which did not suffer from outdated methods of exploitation or the working-out of the more profitable seams. The degree to which individual coalfields depended on precarious export markets also varied, with the new areas tied largely to more stable domestic consumption. Even within the older coalfields there was a very wide range of variation in the viability and efficiency of the different colliery enterprises involved. In the Durham coalfield, for instance, some new or modernized coastal collieries presented a picture of substantial success very different from the serious difficulties facing other pits in the interior of the county. Some of the older coalfields had seen immense development in the half-century or so before 1914, based largely on the existence of export markets which in one form or another, including ships' bunkering, had consumed about a third of the total British coal production before 1914. In the years after 1918 it became increasingly clear that these pre-war markets were not secure, and that the competition of overseas producers was dangerous.

In 1923 the French occupation of the Ruhr coalfield brought a temporary stop to competition from this important rival, and in this fortuitously improved situation for British coal exports the miners' union was able early in 1924 to conclude a much more favourable wage agreement with the owners, which would last until the spring of 1925. Such a fillip, however, could have no significant impact upon the basic problems of obsolescence and imperfect organization which faced large parts, though not all, of this vital element in the British economy.

The successful diplomacy of the 1924 Labour government was a factor in bringing about a French withdrawal from the Ruhr, while the accompanying Dawes plan for the settlement of German reparations brought about the availability of large quantities of German coal at prices with which many British producers could not compete. It was in this bleak situation that the coal industry anticipated the end of the existing wage agreement. Political events at home also altered the situation. The wage revision in 1924 had taken place from the miners' point of view with a friendly Labour government in office. That government had fallen before the end of the year, and at the ensuing general election the Conservatives scored a major victory, winning 419 of the 615 seats and coming very close to capturing an absolute majority of the popular vote. Although the Labour Party lost only forty seats overall, and the Liberals fared much worse, the Conservatives seemed secure in office with a formidable constitutional mandate at the beginning of 1925.

It could hardly be said that the incoming prime minister was to be numbered among organized labour's most determined enemies on the British political scene. Baldwin's character, and his own substantial industrial experience, inclined him towards conciliatory policies. This stance was exemplified in 1925 by his skilful, resolute and successful opposition to an attempt by right-wingers in his own party to secure legislation imposing restrictions on trade unions. However, Baldwin's views were by no means universally shared by all Conservatives; in the new cabinet, on the Conservative back benches in the Commons and in the country there were elements much more opposed to the power of organized labour.

One early decision of the incoming administration played some part in the creation of the 1925–6 crisis. It was decided that Britain would return to the Gold Standard at the pre-war exchange level with effect from 1st May 1925. The reasons for the decision were complex, and in terms of contemporary economic orthodoxy there were good reasons for the step, but the move probably resulted in making British goods more expensive in export markets, and thereby added to the pressures on the vulnerable sectors of the coal industry.

After Black Friday, April 1921, the trade union movement's leadership had been trying to remedy the damage caused by that event by the creation of a more broadly-based and well-organized industrial alliance for mutual support in disputes with employers. A good deal of progress had been made in this direction, but arrangements for effective and reliable co-operation between the autonomous unions with their very varied constitutional arrangements was not easy. Before these negotiations could reach fruition a further crisis erupted in the coal industry with the approaching expiry of the 1924 wage agreement. The owners were determined to cheapen the cost of British coal by reducing the costs of production; in a labour-intensive industry like coal-mining this meant reducing labour costs, in effect reacting to an adverse market situation by reducing the standard of living of the work force involved. At the end of June 1925 the coal owners announced their terms, to take effect late in July. The new terms would certainly have involved substantial cuts in actual earnings.

The miners' union at once appealed to other unions for support in resisting this ultimatum. The response was prompt, and even though the proposed industrial alliance had not yet been consummated there was another body able to take the lead in organizing support. In 1920 the old Parliamentary Committee of the Trades Union Congress had been replaced by the TUC General Council as a central representative body for the trade union movement. The General Council possessed only limited powers, but these included a right to intervene in a dispute which involved 'any vital question of Trade Union principle'. A timely revision of the General Council's Standing Orders, effected in 1924, had strengthened the body's powers to organize support for trade unions involved in disputes where negotiations broke down. In addition the General Council could intervene in a dispute which affected groups of workers beyond those actually parties to the dispute.

On 10th July the miners' executive met the General Council and received full backing in their determination to resist the owners' demands. Acting on behalf of the miners, the leaders of the TUC then approached the government. Baldwin rejected the suggestion that a major and damaging clash could be avoided by the provision of a public subsidy to maintain the existing wage rates for the time being, and no progress was made in these contacts. The TUC then went ahead with arrangements which would have imposed a total embargo on coal movements at the end of July. It now seems clear that the Baldwin government was in a stronger position to face such a confrontation than Lloyd George had occupied in 1920. Contingency plans involving recourse to the Emergency Powers Act existed, although preparations for their implementation were incomplete. Some preparatory work had been carried out under Baldwin's government in 1923, and the 1924 Labour government had not impeded these arrangements, indeed it had shown itself willing to apply the Emergency Powers Act if necessary. From the beginning of Baldwin's second administration, steps had been taken to improve the contingency preparations. Nevertheless, faced with the determination of the TUC to mobilize full-scale support for the miners in the summer of 1925, the Conservative government declined a policy of confrontation and instead acted swiftly to stave off an immediate conflict. At the eleventh hour Baldwin imposed a temporary lull. The owners' notices were withdrawn, a subsidy from public funds would sustain the existing level of wages till the end of April 1926, while in the meantime a further Royal Commission would enquire into the problems of the coal industry and make recommendations for dealing with them. This interim settlement was announced on the afternoon of Friday 31 July 1925, and the success with which organized labour had forced the government into these concessions was commemorated in the term 'Red Friday' in contrast to the 'Black Friday' of 1921.

ATTEMPTS TO AVOID CONFRONTATION

The Royal Commission was small in number, but formidable in membership. It was headed by Sir Herbert Samuel, a distinguished Liberal politician, who was joined by Sir William Beveridge, one of the country's leading experts in matters involving welfare. The other two members were Sir Herbert Lawrence, a distinguished soldier in the First World War and subsequently a prominent banker and Kenneth Lee, an outstandingly successful textile magnate. There was no direct representative of labour on the commission, but its enquiries were skilfully carried out. When their Report appeared early in March, 1926 it included a number of important proposals for the reform of the ailing coal industry. Outright nationalization of the mines was not regarded as necessary or desirable, but nationalization of mining royalties was recommended. A major element in the Report involved far-reaching proposals for the reorganization of the mining industry, with a planned programme of amalgamation and rationalization to eliminate inefficient patterns of production. There were proposals for substantial reforms in current marketing arrangements for coal, for much greater use of scientific research, and for the establishment of a national wages board for the industry. Recommendations were also made for a series of improvements in the field of miners' welfare. At the same time the Report concluded that in the present state of affairs it was impossible to avoid some reduction in wages. The commissioners argued that the continued public subsidization of this one industry was out of the question, and that if production costs were not cut by wage reductions, then the inevitable consequence would be substantial closures among the less profitable collieries.

On 24th March the government announced that it was willing to legislate to give effect to these proposals provided that both sides of the industry agreed to accept them. This agreement was not forthcoming. The owners were not prepared to swallow the Report's recommendations for the reorganization of the industry; the miners refused to accept any proposals which involved reduction in wages or extensions in hours of work. Much of April was consumed in unavailing negotiations between the TUC, the government, miners and owners, and by 23rd April it seemed clear that neither the owners or the miners would budge sufficiently from their entrenched positions for an agreement to be reached. The TUC leadership had maintained their support for the miners while making strenuous efforts to bring about a compromise solution. When the impasse seemed unmistakably plain, the General Council summoned a special conference of trade union executives for 29th April. By the end of April the best terms which the TUC negotiators had been able to extract from the government comprised an undertaking to appoint an 'authoritative inquiry' to follow up the Samuel proposals on reorganization, coupled with a wage cut of about thirteen per cent and raising the maximum working day for face workers to eight hours. These terms were wholly unacceptable to the miners' leaders, who regarded the attainment of the seven-hour day as something which could not be regarded as re-negotiable. At the same time the miners' executive did show some willingness to compromise; they were prepared to consider some wage reduction if this were coupled with cast-iron guarantees for a rapid implementation of far-reaching reorganization of the industry, something which the government had not conceded.

At this point in the complex discussions, developments at the special conference of union executives injected a further urgency into the situation, while with the expiry of the breathing space bought in July 1925 the employers' latest ultimatum to the miners was due to take effect on 1st May. The conference, late on 30th April, heard Arthur Pugh deliver a pessimistic report on the progress of negotiations, and made clear their overwhelming determination to stand by the miners. Meanwhile, a little earlier, the government had acted by proclaiming the existence of a State of Emergency. On Saturday 1st May the leaders of the TUC held an important meeting with the miners' president, Herbert Smith. It seems that the participants in this discussion emerged from it with differing understandings as to what had transpired. The TUC leaders, including their chairman, Pugh, intended to couple with the offer of support to the miners a clear understanding that the miners must now accept that the TUC were in charge of the unions' side of the dispute, and that a settlement might have to include some concession on wages. It seems unlikely that Smith did in fact accept these terms, but his allies seem to have believed that he had done so.

Later on 1st May, with the miners already locked out, the conference of trade union executives, with some 800 members representing 141 separate unions, re-convened. The General Council of the TUC offered resolutions in favour of national industrial action in support of the miners to begin on 3rd May, and for recognizing the General Council as the body responsible for conducting the trade union side of the confrontation. These resolutions were accepted by an overwhelming majority, the

National Union of Seamen being the only union of any size to oppose them. The term 'General Strike' was sedulously avoided in these transactions with such expressions as 'co-ordinated industrial action' being employed instead. The conference then dispersed, leaving the TUC leaders to organize their campaign by the selective calling out of key groups of workers in support of the miners.

Even while these preparations for decisive action were taking place, the TUC leaders persisted in their efforts to bring about a peaceful resolution of the crisis. There still seemed a possibility of compromise arranged around a combination of solid guarantees of reorganization from government and some concession on wages from the miners. Discussions on these lines between negotiating teams from the TUC and the cabinet continued late on 1st May; ministers wanted to confirm that the miners could show flexibility on pay while the union men wished to extract undertakings on reorganization. Late on that evening agreement seemed to come in sight. Pugh, on the strength of his meeting with Herbert Smith earlier in the day, maintained that the miners would be prepared to move on the pay front, and the negotiators then drew up a tentative document summarizing their proposals. The understanding was that Pugh and his fellow-representatives from the General Council would obtain the agreement of the miners' executive and return in readiness for a cabinet meeting to be held at noon the next day.

It now transpired that there had been a failure of communications on the union side. After the ending of the executives' conference the miners' leaders had left London to take up the fight on the various coalfields and could not be reached quickly. A. J. Cook, secretary of the miners' union, was still in London, and he reiterated his opposition to any proposal which involved wage cuts. Of the two mining representatives who were members of the General Council, one was ill and the other absent in Scotland. These developments injected an awkward delay at a critical moment. The cabinet was divided in its attitude to the developing crisis, with Baldwin and his fellow-moderates opposed by such hard-liners as the Chancellor of the Exchequer, Winston Churchill, and the Home Secretary, Sir William Joynson-Hicks. The hard-liners were strengthened by the situation they met when the cabinet duly convened at noon on Sunday 2nd May. The expected TUC reply was not forthcoming, and it was nearly two hours before ministers learned of the miners' absence, which was the cause of the delay. The cabinet also learned that strike notices had already gone out, including those to branches of the rail unions. It was not until later that day that effective negotiations could be resumed, and 11 p.m. before the miners' representatives arrived at 11 Downing Street to discuss with the TUC men the progress made the previous night. The latter had already sensed a less conciliatory atmosphere on the government side, with a distinct suggestion of a stiffening of terms in that quarter.

While the union teams were negotiating at 11 Downing Street a cabinet official arrived to ask the TUC leaders to see the prime minister. When Pugh and his colleagues met Baldwin they were dismayed to receive an intimation that negotiations were at an end; 'overt action' had taken place, and the government now declined any further discussions without an explicit withdrawal of the threat of a national strike. A relatively trivial event had tipped the scales within the divided cabinet. A group of workers at the *Daily Mail* had flatly refused to print a hostile editorial entitled 'For King and Country' and pleas from their own union officials had failed to move them to desist from this precipitate action. This could of course be seen by the cabinet hard-liners as 'overt action' involving deliberate censorship while negotiations were still proceeding. At Downing Street the TUC representatives were completely taken aback by this wholly unexpected development. After adjourning for a hasty discussion the chairman and secretary of the General Council, Pugh and Citrine, returned to Downing Street to try to patch things up, only to find that the prime minister had retired to bed. When Ernest Bevin tried to obtain the re-opening of negotiations later on 3rd May he found both miners and government unwilling to budge—the miners evinced no willingness to compromise, while the government now stood firm on its determination to refuse to be coerced by the threat of a general strike. By the end of the day it was plain that the efforts to forestall the national stoppage by negotiation had failed.

STRIKERS VERSUS GOVERNMENT

The dispute was now essentially a confrontation between the established national government and the trade union movement. There can be no doubt which side was better prepared for the crisis.

During the time bought by the 1925 interim settlement the government's contingency plans had been carefully elaborated, so that by May 1926 all that was necessary to bring them into operation was a cabinet decision. The country was to be divided into ten regions, and for each region a junior minister and supporting staff had been earmarked in advance; the principal task of these groups was to maintain essential supplies such as food and fuel. In London the Home Office operated as a centre of communications and advice. On the whole the contingency arrangements worked well, though it is by no means clear whether the arrangements for transport and supply would have been able to cope with a longer struggle. In addition to the government's own resources, it could call on the services of very many volunteers willing to rally to the side of established authority in the crisis. The main volunteer grouping was the Organization for the Maintenance of Supplies; this organization was built up in the months before the General Strike and, while it was basically an unofficial initiative, some government encouragement was given to it. In the event the OMS was probably more important as a propaganda element than for any effectiveness with which its volunteers could replace skilled strikers.

The position on the trade union side was very different. The leaders of the TUC had plainly pinned their hopes to the chances of a peaceful settlement of the mining dispute, and had been anxious to avoid any overt preparations which might have appeared as a provocation to the Conservative government. No one has ever suggested that the TUC leaders were spoiling for a fight. Indeed, events at both the TUC and Labour Party conferences in 1925 pointed in other directions. At the TUC the normal workings of trade union representation on the General Council had produced a membership more inclined to moderate and conciliatory courses than their predecessors. At the Labour Party conference, while a number of innocuous left-wing resolutions on international affairs were accepted, a much more important decision was taken which showed the hostility of the established trade union leadership towards militant dissent. The application of the Communist Party for affiliation to the Labour Party had been rejected earlier; now most of the union block votes were cast to exclude individual communists from participation in the Labour Party's affairs.

When the crunch came at the beginning of May 1926, no effective preparations had been made to enable the General Council of the TUC to carry out the supervisory role on which it had insisted so strongly during the conference of union executives. The lack of preparation was damaging to efficiency, but the nature of the British trade union movement made the weakness somewhat less wounding than might at first sight appear. The movement was not a centralized organization, but much more a voluntary grouping of autonomous societies. It was naturally assumed that the TUC leadership would work through the established machinery of the individual unions. Although there was some confusion, and the period of the strike was marked by defective communications on the union side, the manner in which the strike was made effective testified to the strength of the unions. The General Council acted through individual unions to bring out on 4th May a first range of groups of key workers, including those employed in railways, road transport, ports, printing, chemicals, iron and steel, electricity, gas and important sections of the building industry. The response to the strike call was dramatic, the solidarity unmistakable. One of the best-known examples was provided by the workers of the biggest railway network, the London, Midland and Scottish Railway. All but 207 of its 15,062 engine drivers obeyed the call, all but 62 of the 14,143 firemen and all but 153 of the 9,979 guards. The amount of rail traffic, still the crucial element in internal transport, remained throughout the strike derisively small, despite the inflated claims made by the government's propaganda. The solidarity of the railway workers was by no means unusual.

The second factor which compensated for the lack of organized preparation on the union side was the initiative and determination shown by the strike leadership at local level. Often left without much in the way of effective guidance from the centre, local strike committees, usually dominated by representatives of local branches of individual unions, embarked upon a wide range of activities with a great deal of confidence and success. Some of them organized their own communication links with London, using couriers to report on their own situation and obtain advice and instructions. A careful watch was maintained to ensure the continued solidarity of the stoppage. Attempts were made, with varying degrees of completeness, to organize a supervised system of permits which might conciliate public opinion by facilitating the movement of foodstuffs without seriously compromising the efficiency of the strike in other ways. In many cases the local committees set about the organization of welfare and recreational activities for the benefit of their supporters.

Those who took the lead in these local strike committees were men with long experience of militant union activities, but it would be wrong to see them in any generalized way as agencies of revolutionary objectives. There were, however, those who saw in the crisis a marvellous opportunity to bring about a revolutionary organization of the working class for much wider purposes than support of the miners in the present dispute. A good example was cited by Baines and Bean in their study of the general strike on Merseyside, where the communist J. T. Murphy had this to say when the general strike began:

Let us be clear what a general strike means. It can only mean the throwing down of the gauntlet to the capitalist state, and all the powers at its disposal. Either that challenge is only a gesture, in which case the capitalist class will not worry about it, or it must develop its challenge into an actual fight for power, in which case we land into civil war. Any leaders who talk about a general strike without facing this obvious fact are bluffing both themselves and the workers.

This was not, however, the dominant attitude on the trade union side. The allegiance of the overwhelming majority of those involved in the strike was not an attachment to revolutionary theories of society but a loyalty to the trade union movement, and especially to its constituent sectional organizations. Even in this crisis examples were to be found of officials of individual unions resisting attempts by local strike committees to interfere with the autonomy of individual societies. The idea of the confrontation developing into 'an actual fight for power' possessed only very limited acceptance.

It was an idea abhorrent to the moderate leadership of the TUC. They had entertained high hopes that the threat to employ their industrial strength on such a massive scale would have sufficed to bring about some compromise solution to the mining dispute, and had not reckoned on the conflict escalating into a major constitutional issue. The government's position now was a relatively simple one. For any organization to paralyse the national economy in order to force its will on the elected Parliament and government of the nation was a challenge to constitutional order and legitimacy which could not be tolerated. Baldwin steadily maintained his refusal to enter into any further negotiations on the coal industry's problems unless the coercion embodied in the General Strike was called off unconditionally. At the same time the prime minister sought to limit the conflict by adopting a generally conciliatory stance in other ways. He rejected proposals from his own hard-line colleagues which might have resulted in major provocations to the strikers. With rare exceptions the armed forces were employed sparingly and unobtrusively, and while remaining adamant on the main constitutional issue Baldwin adopted a public front of sweet reasonableness. He was well aware of the reluctance with which the TUC leaders had embarked upon a major confrontation with the government. At the same time he was not prepared to allow others to take initiatives which might imperil the government's insistence on the unconditional withdrawal of the coercive general strike. For this reason the government refused to allow the Archbishop of Canterbury to broadcast a plea for a compromise solution which would have involved government concessions as part of a plan for ending the strike. When Baldwin himself spoke on the BBC on the evening of Saturday 8th May, however, he was carefully unprovocative:

The Trades Union Congress have only to cancel the General Strike and we shall immediately begin with the utmost care and patience with them again the long laborious task which has been proceeding over these many weeks, of endeavouring to rebuild on an economic foundation the prosperity of the coal trade. . . . I am a man of peace. I am longing and working and praying for peace. But I will not surrender the safety and the security of the British Constitution. You placed me in power eighteen months ago by the largest majority accorded any party for many, many years. Have I done anything to forfeit that confidence? Cannot you trust me to ensure a square deal for the parties—to secure even justice between man and man?

The principal objective of the TUC negotiators had been from the beginning to secure a solution to the coal crisis rather than bring about a first-class constitutional crisis. They still hoped that some kind of acceptable agreement could be reached, and were anxious to find some channel by which constructive discussions might be reopened. After various false starts, a promising possibility seemed to be offered by the intervention of Sir Herbert Samuel, ex-chairman of the 1925–6 Royal Commission. He had been abroad when the General Strike broke out, but at once returned home to see if he could help in any way to resolve the dispute. From the beginning the cabinet was informed of his activities, but made it plain to him that the government would not budge from its determination that the calling-off of the strike was a prerequisite for further negotiations. No attempt was made to impede his endeavours, but it was made very clear to him that his initiative must be entirely personal and unofficial and that he had no powers to bind the government. For his part Samuel was explicit on this point with the union leaders with whom he made contact. By 6th May he had initiated discussions with TUC leaders, and especially with J. H. Thomas of the National Union of Railwaymen. Thomas had been one of the union leaders much involved in calling off the joint Triple Alliance action on the Black Friday of 1921, and he was now anxious to see the end of the 1926 crisis, believing that a continuation of the General Strike was unlikely to bring any significant gains, while it could involve very considerable peril to the trade union movement as he envisaged it. Samuel's talks with Thomas and other TUC leaders went on from 6th to 10th May. During this period the strike remained solid. Indeed on 7th May the General Council acted to increase the strike's pressure, by issuing orders to call out a second rank of workers, including those in shipbuilding and engineering, with effect from 10th May. The discussions with Samuel essentially represented a continuation of the negotiations which the TUC leaders had earlier held with the government, and centred on trying to find some kind of guarantee for effective reorganization of the coal industry. By 10th May the talks crystallized into the production by Samuel of a memorandum of possible terms for a settlement, including a positive commitment to a far-reaching organization scheme. The TUC negotiators were prepared to accept this document as a suitable basis for further discussions and tried hard to sell the scheme to the miners' executive. Again the miners' leaders proved less than tactful in their handling of their union allies, and brusquely rejected the Samuel memorandum on the evening of 10th May. After further discussions the leaders of the General Council pressed the miners to say that they would accept the document as a basis for further negotiation, with the implicit threat that the continuance of the national sympathetic strike was at stake if the miners refused to accept the advice of the TUC leaders. The miners' leaders asked in return what guarantee they could have that the government would implement the terms of the document, and to this they could be given no satisfactory answer. They therefore persisted in their refusal to see in the memorandum any reliable basis on which to move towards a possible settlement.

It was by now late on 11th May, and at this point the TUC leaders received a message from the prime minister's secretary asking if there was any news on progress for the government. The TUC leaders conferred again briefly and then telephoned to Downing Street to ask for an appointment with the prime minister for midday on 12th May. They had in fact determined to call off the General Strike in the belief that this was now the only way in which any progress towards resolving the crisis could be made. There were some other reasons. The continuance of the strike had been marked by sporadic violence, with something over 3,000 arrests being made overall during the nine days of the strike, mostly concentrated in the key industrial and mining areas. For most historians the limited amount of violence which occurred has seemed remarkable, but it was enough to worry union leaders concerned to avoid any escalation in the scale of serious conflict. Reports had also reached the TUC leaders suggesting that there were signs of weakening in the strike's solidarity, though in fact returns to work were relatively trivial in their extent and impact upon the strike's effectiveness. The main reason for the surrender, however, was the effect on the TUC leaders of the government's adamant stand on the constitutional issue and the belief that a continuance of the strike would do nothing to secure the objectives with which it had been begun.

THE CONSEQUENCES OF THE STRIKE'S COLLAPSE

The government had insisted that the strike must be called off without preconditions and this is what effectively happened. When Pugh and his colleagues had informed Baldwin of the decision to end the strike they had secured no commitments at all on behalf of the government, despite an attempt by Ernest Bevin to tie Baldwin down to guarantees for re-employment and avoidance of victimization. The news that the general strike was over was greeted with a good deal of rejoicing, but also considerable bewilderment among many of the rank and file of the strikers. The TUC leaders were beset by delegations and other representations from the more militant groups, and sought as far as possible to conceal the extent to which the end of the strike amounted to unconditional surrender to the government. In practice each union was left to make the best of its position. Some of them, including the railwaymen and the transport workers, had to resort to further separate industrial action to protect their members against victimization, without complete success.

The sense of betrayal was especially acute among the miners, now left to maintain their obdurate resistance in isolation. This may be a little too sweeping, for the end of the General Strike did, as the government had promised, open the way for a resumption of negotiations on the problems of the coal industry. These efforts dragged on for months, but foundered again and again on the same refusal of both miners and owners to move from their entrenched positions. The owners, although their opinion was not united, would not accept a far-reaching programme of compulsory reorganization of the industry, and the government was not willing to coerce them. The miners' leaders were almost as inflexible in their determination to defend the standard of living of their supporters, irrespective of any other considerations. In this there can be no doubt that they merely reflected the overwhelming majority of their followers. Baldwin tried repeatedly to obtain an agreed solution, but his freedom of action was limited and his main legislative intervention was not calculated to conciliate the miners. By statute the maximum working day for face workers was raised from seven to eight hours.

The miners' cause appeared increasingly bleak as the weeks dragged on. In some places where Poor Law authorities depended heavily on mining votes, this source of help was for some time exploited to help the miners, in the teeth of the relevant regulations. However, the Ministry of Health acted to check such disobedience, and in the case of the Chester-le-Street Union, where the defiance of regulations had been especially flagrant, used new statutory powers to supersede the elected guardians and replace them by its own nominees. There was a good deal of charitable activity in support of mining families, but such palliatives could not prolong resistance indefinitely. In early September, however, less than one in twenty of Britain's miners had given up the struggle and returned to work. There were some cracks in the fabric of miners' unity. In many coalfields the numbers returning to the pits were trivial, but in some cases, especially the Nottinghamshire and Derbyshire coalfields, the situation was different. This breach was to culminate in late November in the creation of a breakaway Nottinghamshire miners' union which made its own arrangements with the local owners for a return to work. For the most part, however, the miners stayed firm, and during the autumn their executive rejected a number of proposals which would have involved considerable concessions on their original stand on hours and wages. In mid-November the miners' leaders were brought to acceptance of defeat, and a special Miners' Federation delegate conference reluctantly decided to recommend their followers to accept the government's latest offer, which presented some concessions in detail, such as the creation of District Boards for each mining area, with independent chairmen, to fix terms of employment. This decision, reached by a narrow majority, was followed by a ballot in which the miners voted by 460,806 to 313,200 to reject the terms, with many of the older coalfields strongly for rejection of arrangements which would have left them especially vulnerable to reductions. The majority for resistance was by now clearly waning, and the miners' conference decided to accept that the main battle was lost. By 29th November work had been resumed in most coalfields. The pits in Yorkshire and South Wales re-opened on 30th November. In County Durham a pithead ballot still returned a narrow majority against accepting the terms offered by the local employers, but in view of the narrowness of the vote the county federation accepted the need for a return to work. The terms of settlement varied from district to district; in County Durham, for instance, coal hewers came back to a seven-and-a-half hour day instead of the previous seven hours, and the new legal maximum of eight hours was not imposed.

The decision to return to work was a source of immediate relief to many miners and their families, though for some of them the settlement brought nothing, for not all pits re-opened and not all the striking miners were re-employed. On the other hand, the long dispute engendered a further spirit of rankling bitterness into the already troubled industry. It is sometimes said that the miners had been starved back to work. In any literal sense of the word this is something of an exaggeration. Mining families had, however, endured months of deprivation, with a very low standard of living when compared with their normal life, with months also of cumulative boredom and frustration for the majority of those involved. They were conscious of the isolation in which they had been placed by the end of the General Strike. They received numerous expressions of sympathy, and contributions to funds from a variety of sources both at home and abroad, but no aid which could effectively enable them to win their fight. Coal imports into Britain, reaching some four million tons by October, limited the impact of the mining strike on fuel supplies, and no effective action was taken by other workers to impede this flow.

After the events of May there was a major inquest within the trade union movement. The TUC leaders sought to evade the many accusations levelled against them, and displayed considerable skill in defending their action in ending the General Strike. This is not surprising, for men did not rise to become leaders of major unions without exhibiting or acquiring considerable dexterity. J. H. Thomas, for example, was under attack at the annual delegate conference of the National Union of Railwaymen in early July 1926, and in his history of the union Professor Bagwell has shown how Thomas skilfully outmanoeuvred his militant opponents and brought the meeting to agree by a two to one majority 'that having heard the report in relation to the calling-off of the General Strike by the TUC we accept the explanation given'.

The main inquest was postponed to a special conference to be held in January 1927. The TUC leaders would have welcomed an opportunity to vindicate their actions earlier, but agreed to the delay at the wish of the miners' executive, even though relations between the two groups remained distinctly strained. The special TUC conference was called 'to consider the report of the General Council on the National Strike'. At this meeting the decision to call off the strike was bitterly attacked by the miners and by their supporters, while the TUC leaders accused the miners' leaders of a fatal obstinacy and inflexibility, and a refusal to abide by the earlier decision to concede management of the dispute to the General Council. In the event the report of the General Council was accepted by a vote of 2,840,000 to 1,095,000.

The failure of the General Strike ushered in a period of great difficulty for the trade unions, with serious drops in membership and resources continuing well into the next decade and accompanied by the effects of severe economic depression and mass unemployment. There were attempts by militants, outraged by the circumstances in which the May strike had ended, to oust the existing leadership and in some cases even to create breakaway militant unions, but these achieved little success. Men like Thomas and Bevin were not easily ousted, and many of the TUC leaders of 1926 still held key union positions for long afterwards.

The role of the government in the aftermath of the General Strike was much less than glorious. Legislation aimed at mining reorganization was enacted, but without the inclusion of the compulsion which could alone have made the measure effective. In 1927 Baldwin felt unable to repeat his refusal of two years earlier to sanction legislative action against the trade union movement inspired by his hard-line followers and colleagues. The 1927 Trade Disputes and Trade Union Act forbade civil service unions to be affiliated to the TUC, tried to outlaw sympathetic strikes by limiting participation to workers in the enterprises directly concerned in a dispute, and sought also to outlaw strikes aimed at coercing the government by inflicting hardship on the community. In addition the Act imposed a requirement that payment of the political levy to the Labour Party by members of an affiliated union must be the result of a deliberate 'contracting in', instead of the 'contracting out' arrangements usual before. The 1927 Act had little effect in practice, but aroused lasting bitterness within the trade union movement. Its triumphant repeal was one of the first actions of the victorious Labour Party after the 1945 general election. Nationalization of the coal mines was to be another.

Six

St Helens 1970

The 1970 strike by glass workers employed by the Pilkington group based on St Helens is a particularly well documented and interesting strike. In addition to the report of an official Court of Inquiry we have a valuable account derived from two lecturers from Liverpool University who maintained a careful and meticulous survey of the course of the dispute.

The company involved was both an old and a markedly successful one. The Pilkington family were engaged in glass-making at St Helens for some years before Victoria ascended the throne. By the mid-nineteenth century the family firm was well established as one of the dominant elements in the United Kingdom glass industry. A high level of managerial competence in both the commercial and technical spheres was commonly present in the company's affairs. In addition, for many years the firm enjoyed a considerable reputation for enlightened dealings with its work force. This was not an uninterrupted success—for example there was a major strike of some skilled men in 1870 which lasted six months—but by the beginning of the twentieth century Pilkingtons prided themselves on a continuous tradition of paternalism exemplified by the early provision of such benefits as recreational, educational and medical services for their employees. As in many other areas, the First World War brought further advances in industrial relations. The company gave formal recognition in 1917 to the National Amalgamation of Labour, one of the forerunners of the National Union of General and Municipal Workers

(NUGMW). In the following year, under some government prodding, the company set up a Joint Industrial Council; on this body company and union representatives sat together to sort out problems relating to industrial relations throughout the Pilkington Group's plants. The Council was composed of twenty-two company representatives, seven full-time union officials and fifteen elected workers, together with a secretary.

This system may well have appeared sensible and sophisticated in 1918, but half a century later there were ominous signs of creaking. The centralizing of significant negotiations in this sphere brought advantages in the first instance, but some accompanying disadvantages were becoming apparent by the 1960s. Although the Pilkington Group's size, and the number of its work force, had continued to grow, there had been no radical alterations in the firm's industrial relations machinery, and the Joint Industrial Council had grown to be uncomfortably remote from many of the firm's employees. It was common for elections of worker members of the Council to arouse little interest, and communications between this key body and the shop floor were increasingly tenuous.

The Pilkington management continued in the mid-twentieth century a markedly successful policy of expansion, but it seems likely that preoccupation with commercial and technical success was not accompanied by a like emphasis on a careful watch on the company's industrial relations. Indeed, some of the later annexations brought with them problems which were not completely appreciated by the company's leaders. By 1965 the Triplex Safety Glass Company Limited was a Pilkington subsidiary, and in 1967 Pilkingtons also annexed the only other large supplier of safety glass to the British motor industry. The takeover of Triplex involved the absorption into the Pilkington empire of a company in which industrial relations had taken a course markedly different from the centralized bargaining system adopted by Pilkingtons since 1918. The conventions at Triplex had laid a much greater weight on shop floor and individual plant bargaining, and the leaders of the Triplex workers had been notably reluctant to see these conventions buried in the Pilkington Joint Industrial Council system. From time to time in the later 1960s there were rumblings of discontent among the 1,200 or so workers at the Triplex plant at St Helens. Even before the 1970 strike erupted, the Triplex men had been trying to obtain the establishment of a separate union branch for themselves, disliking a situation in which they existed only as a distinct minority in a larger branch.

Other features of industrial relations within the Pilkington Group's increasingly complex structure provided opportunities for trouble by the 1960s. A full revision of the firm's wage structure was long overdue, for successive tinkerings since 1933 had left payments based upon an increasingly complicated array of basic wages and bonus arrangements which could produce misunderstandings and anomalies from which friction and resentment could easily arise.

If there were possible sources of trouble on the company side of industrial relations, much the same situation existed on the union side. The National Union of General and Municipal Workers seemed to occupy a very strong position as the accredited representative of the overwhelming majority of Pilkington workers. In 1964 the close co-operation between Pilkingtons and the union seemed sealed with an agreement which gave the NUGMW a post-entry closed shop, while the company agreed to act as the union's agent in deducting union dues from wages. Nevertheless there were serious weaknesses in the union's position. The growth of Pilkingtons and of union membership had not been paralleled by a related reorganization and instead about 7,400 glass workers were enrolled in one mammoth NUGMW branch, No. 91, at St Helens. Although this branch regularly contributed around £40,000 yearly in union subscriptions, it was furnished with only one full-time secretary. There were serious deficiencies in communications between the union and its mass membership. Although there were about 120 accredited shop stewards in the Pilkington plants at St Helens, not more than about twenty of them were likely to turn up at meetings to transact branch business, while attendance from other members was normally on an even smaller scale. While the NUGMW was one of the unions which tried to maintain a tight control over the autonomy of the local branches, this was not matched by an adequate staff and an adequate concern to see that communication with shop floor opinion was sedulously maintained. These organizational problems were obvious enough by the late 1960s, and discussions had already been initiated with a view to reorganizing No. 91, but no great urgency had been shown and nothing effective achieved by the time of the 1970 strike.

UNOFFICIAL ACTION

If it had not been for these underlying factors it is unlikely that the original cause of the dispute would have developed into a major conflict lasting seven weeks. Previous months had seen evidence of sporadic discontent among some elements of the Pilkington workers at least, with demands for substantial wage increases very much in the air. Then on the afternoon of Friday 3rd April 1970 trouble came to a head in the Flat Drawn glass shop inside the biggest of the Pilkington plants at St Helens. In this area the work conditions were uncomfortable and tedious, and there was an unusually high turnover rate of employees; the subsequent Court of Inquiry ascertained that thirty-three of the original forty-five strikers in this shop had worked there for less than one year. Furnace heat provided conditions in which irritability could easily be provoked, and the shop had a reputation in the works as a centre of discontent. In the previous week there had been a complaint there that some of the men had been underpaid as a result of a miscalculation of bonus payments, and now on 3rd April it seemed that the same thing had happened again. While attempts were being made to sort this out, and tempers were still running high, some of the men remembered a wage claim which they had already put forward and began to voice demands for an increase of 2s.6d. an hour, a claim which this group of workers had tried unsuccessfully to press upon No. 91 branch a little while earlier. While shop stewards, union officials and management representatives were trying to cool the situation, resentment exploded in an immediate walk-out, now expressed in terms of this wage claim rather than the original bonus grievance.

Management, union officials and even the majority of the men involved were taken by surprise by the speed of developments. Before the end of the day the walk-out had spread to a second Pilkington plant near by, and the weekend saw further important but essentially confused developments. On the Saturday morning about eighty shop stewards came together in a branch meeting to consider what to do. It was obvious enough at this meeting that the walk-out was a direct breach of the conciliation procedures agreed with the company, and against union policy. However, groups of the more militant strikers were already at work on the men at the other four Pilkington plants at St Helens, and when the shop stewards repaired to their own places of work they found themselves faced with a difficult situation in which they felt that they could not come out in open opposition to the walk-out. In effect this left many of the rank-and-file members of the union under the impression that the union condoned the strike. A mass meeting on Sunday decided that the strike was to continue and by the next morning all six Pilkington plants at St Helens were involved. This had been effected by crowds of strikers from the plants first affected visiting the other four sites and chanting such slogans as 'All out, £5 now'. During the next few days the outbreak spread to seven of the eleven Pilkington plants in other parts of the country.

The strike represented a plain breach of the union's own rules, as well as the procedural agreements with the employers. The rules of the NUGMW carefully reserved to the union's central leadership the right to authorize strike action on such a scale. The vigour of the unofficial walk-out therefore faced union officials with a difficult situation. To the local officers the most obvious solution was to have the strike declared official and vindicate the union's leadership of the dispute. Headquarters steadfastly refused to allow the local men to flout the rule book successfully and involve the union in unnecessary trouble with the employers. Faced with a blank refusal by the union's legal authority, the local officials resorted to the subterfuge of declaring the strike 'official at branch level'—an expedient sufficiently transparent to anyone acquainted with the union's constitution and traditions, but capable of influencing the very large number of St Helens members whose connection with the union had been so tenuous.

THE UNION'S REACTION

The next few days saw continued efforts by the union's agents to regain control of the situation. The national official responsible for members in the glass industry, a job he had only recently taken over, faced a mass meeting of strikers on Wednesday 8th April. His object was to persuade the men to return to work and allow the union to pursue their claims and grievances through the agreed negotiating procedures. This was a crucial confrontation for the course of the dispute, for this first intervention by national union authority provided the best chance for the restoration of normality. It was unsuccessful. While the strike's keenest supporters were well-known local men, the national officer was little known and not in the first rank of platform orators. He had to try to explain why the union could not make the strike official, and this could be seen as an unsympathetic letting-down of the local men by the distant central authority. The meeting was in no mood to accept such an unpalatable message. The national official was given a rough reception and his advice for a return to work decisively rejected.

At the same time the union leadership had been trying to set on foot negotiations with Pilkingtons which might produce concessions sufficient to calm the situation. The company's public stance was that it would not negotiate without a return to work and the restoration of the agreed conciliation procedures, but in private the firm was more conciliatory. The union's representatives on the Joint Industrial Council adopted the claim for a £5 wage increase, and the employers agreed to enter into discussions. However, while these negotiations were under way, a significant new element further eroded the union's hold on the situation, with the emergence of an unofficial committee of strike leaders, styled the 'Rank and File Strike Committee', as an alternative centre of leadership. About one-third of this committee came from the shop floor leadership at the Triplex plant.

By 20th April the discussions on the Joint Industrial Council had produced an offer from the firm of a flat £3 per week wage increase, together with an agreement to carry out a full revision of the pay structure as soon as possible. Union officials felt that this offer would be sufficient to bring about a return to work. On the morning of 21st April the proposition was brought before a branch meeting at which a large number of shop stewards were present. This meeting gave the agreement a considerable measure of welcome, but the branch agreed to put the terms before a mass meeting to be held later that day. At the mass meeting the hopes for a speedy settlement to the dispute proved over-optimistic. There was vociferous opposition, and the unofficial leadership made no attempt to support the union's efforts to bring about the end of the strike. Again the union's official representative was unable to sway opinion, and the meeting threw out the proffered terms. The response of the Pilkington plants in other areas was different, and they accepted the agreement and returned to work over the next few days.

At St Helens, however, the unofficial strike continued in full force, with much of the heat concentrated on the conflict between the union and the unofficial leadership which for the time being at least had wrested control from the official union organization. At a further mass meeting on 24th April the principal union spokesman was shouted down. After another excited mass meeting on 29th April a crowd of militant strikers invaded the NUGMW office in St Helens in an unruly fashion and the office was subsequently closed down, adding further to problems of communication between the union's officers and their St Helens membership. In early May intensive picketing frustrated attempts by union supporters to return to work, and these incidents were surrounded by a blaze of publicity from press, radio and television.

As happens not uncommonly in such contexts, there were rumours that the unofficial strike had been fomented and was being maintained by subversive political elements. Members of militant left-wing political groups did turn up at St Helens, and the strike received very sympathetic coverage in the publications emanating from such organizations. It seems unlikely, however, that this provided a major element in the course of the dispute. The militant strike leadership also included men whose political views gave a markedly left-wing tone to the Rank and File Strike Committee's own propaganda about the strike, but it seems unlikely that outside influences played any very significant role.

On 4th May the unofficial strike committee asked the Minister of Employment and Productivity in the Labour Government, Mrs Barbara Castle, to intervene in the dispute, and the minister responded with the appointment of an official Court of Inquiry on 9th May. The report of this Inquiry was to provide an important source for the history of the dispute and its underlying causes, but by the time this report appeared in June it had been overtaken by events.

The conflict between strike leadership and the union continued to escalate. At a mass meeting of strikers on 10th May there was a distribution of forms instructing the employers to discontinue the deduction of union dues from wages, a practice which depended on the workers' agreement to the regular deductions. Effectively the strike leaders were inviting their followers to opt out of the NUGMW, something which was in itself a breach of the 1964 closed shop agreement. Although many of these forms were completed, it does not seem as if at any time this drastic action was implemented by a majority of the men involved in the strike, and there were many who took no very active part in the dispute.

The NUGMW did not favour the mass meeting as an acceptable method of debate and decision. An attempt by the union to obtain a ballot of members during the early stages of the strike had proved abortive, and the results had not been published. Continuing attempts at conciliation produced a second ballot on 16th May, and in this case the exercise was provided with impartial backing by enlisting local clergymen to participate in its organization and supervision. Well over six thousand workers voted, and the result showed a narrow majority in favour of a return to work. The unofficial strike leadership, however, declared that there had been flaws in the procedure adopted and refused to accept the verdict as validly representing the views of their followers.

THE ROLE OF THE TUC AND THE GOVERNMENT

Understandably the national leadership of the trade union movement was concerned at the nature and duration of this conflict and 19th May saw TUC intervention. Vic Feather, the TUC General Secretary, attempted to mediate. He occupied a position of considerable authority and prestige within the trade union movement and his intervention was an important new factor. His proposed terms, however, were scarcely attractive to the unofficial leadership at St Helens. He insisted that a resumption of work was necessary before progress in conciliation could be made, but offered that if the stoppage ended, talks between the unofficial leaders and the NUGMW would be arranged under the aegis of the TUC, with a view to composing their differences. The Rank and File Strike Committee did not find these terms attractive, but put them without any formal recommendation to two mass meetings of their followers held on Wednesday 20th May. The TUC General Secretary refused an invitation to come to St Helens, preferring to exercise the influence of his position and his reputation without a personal appearance on the scene of the dispute. The meetings of 20th May rejected the Feather proposals, but the unofficial leaders knew that their position had been weakened by the earlier rejection of the ballot result and the present rejection of the TUC intervention. At a meeting of the Rank and File Strike Committee on the morning of 21st May it was decided to call a further mass meeting and face it with a positive recommendation in favour of accepting the TUC proposal. At the mass meeting called later the same day this advice was overwhelmingly accepted, and the strike was called off.

The official Court of Inquiry had been holding its investigations at the same time as these exchanges had taken place, but its formal report was not completed until 10th June. The report included criticisms of all three major elements in the affair, the company, the union and the unofficial leadership. The failure both of Pilkingtons and the NUGMW to ensure that their administrative arrangements corresponded to the needs of the situation was pointed out. During the Inquiry the union had criticized the frequent recourse to mass meetings of strikers—'Mass meetings were not the most appropriate settings for discussing detailed arrangements'. The court accepted this attitude in its report—'The use of the open-air mass meeting as the principal organ of decision-making proved unsatisfactory and disruptive'; in addition the court noted the difficulty caused at such meetings by 'rowdy elements in the crowd, perhaps intent on disrupting the meeting' in connection with the rejection of the earlier peace-making moves. The report noticed also and disapproved of the failure to publish the result of the first, union organized, ballot held on 20th April, which was widely believed to have shown a majority against a return to work.

The most severe criticisms in the report, however, were reserved for the unofficial strike leaders. Their refusal to accept the 16th May ballot verdict was, for instance, said to demonstrate 'lack of mature judgement and sound leadership'. The report concluded that:

Above all the situation in which Union members set themselves against the Union must end and the energies of those who disapprove of past practices by the Union must be bent to see that they play a full part in the Union so that what they criticized is not allowed to arise again.

These hopes were not to be realized, at least in the immediate aftermath. The talks between union representatives and the St Helens Rank and File Strike Committee under TUC auspices duly took place, with Vic Feather acting as chairman. The unofficial leaders had several objectives. They wanted to be represented on any future NUGMW negotiations with Pilkington, they wished to establish the principle (contrary to NUGMW conventions) that all agreements reached should be subject to the consent of the mass of the members involved, and they demanded new elections for the union side of the Joint Industrial Council. None of these demands was acceptable to the union, which in its turn demanded the cessation of the abusive attacks on the union emanating from the St Helens militants. The talks speedily broke down without any sign of agreement having been reached.

Since the breach between the St Helens unofficial strike leaders and the NUGMW seemed irreconcilable, the former tried to find some other relevant established union to provide an alternative legitimate home for them. Their first choice was the other great general union, the Transport and General Workers' Union, which already had a foothold in the glass industry, including an important Triplex plant outside St Helens. There was never any real chance of this switch of allegiance being allowed. The trade union movement had a long-standing internal agreement against the 'poaching' of members, and while there have been some examples of successful switches of allegiance, they have been few and far between. Moreover the TGWU had its own history of trouble with militant dissidents within its ranks and its leadership was unlikely to welcome others with open arms.

Faced with their failure to obtain an alternative home with an established union, the militant leaders at St Helens went on to pursue the forlorn hope of creating a new breakaway union based on their own following, the Glass and General Workers' Union. This move took place early in June, but even at its inception less than half of the old membership of the NUGMW branch could be persuaded to join the new organization, and many of these took no active part in the affairs of the new union. The high hopes with which the new society was founded never reached fruition. There were plans for a much extended coverage, and some expressions of sympathy from other elements in the trade union movement, but nothing very concrete issued from these. From the beginning the breakaway union faced hostility from the NUGMW, the bulk of the established leadership of the trade union movement, and the employers. The NUGMW naturally embarked upon a strenuous counter-attack; the old union still possessed a substantial nucleus of support among the St Helens workers and was able to obtain a considerable success in winning back dissidents into the fold. Attempts by the leaders of the new union to force Pilkingtons to accept the Glass and General Workers' as the accredited representative of many glass workers culminated in a disastrous attempt at further strike action in August 1970 which succeeded in bringing out only a few hundred workers. The company had no intention of yielding, and could now insist that any re-employment of the strikers must be dependent upon their acceptance of the established conditions of employment, including the mandatory NUGMW membership prescribed by the 1964 closed shop agreement.

With these events the main course of the 1970 dispute was over, and the militant leaders had failed in their attempts to translate their temporary ascendancy of the early summer into a long-term established position of leadership. Pilkingtons and the NUGMW were left with the task of absorbing the lessons which had been so painfully administered, and taking steps to remedy the deficiencies of organization, communication and planning which had provided so much of the underlying material for the eruption.

Seven

Conclusions

In discussing the history of industrial disputes it is important to stress that we are dealing with a complex phenomenon, and that it is misleading to try to impose on the subject any concepts of simplicity of uniformity. Strikes and other forms of industrial disputes, such as a go-slow or a work-to-rule, can present a kaleidoscopic variety of causes and subsequent events. It is unlikely that the historian will be able to comprehend all the elements involved in even a single dispute, though of course this limitation is by no means confined to this particular area of human behaviour. Nevertheless, within this pattern of variability there are some factors which can be distinguished either because they constantly recur over a long time span or because they have exercised a widespread influence in some specific period. It is convenient to look again at some of these influential factors, examining some elements which can be discerned at work in many disputes stretching over a long period of time, and then some important changes wrought by more general developments during the enormous social transformation which has taken place over the last two centuries.

There are some causes of industrial disputes which have endured throughout the period covered here. It is interesting that our two earliest examples, the two strikes of merchant seamen in 1792 and 1815, were essentially sparked off on the one hand by the perennial problem of the maintenance of real wages at a time of steeply rising prices, and on the other by what was in essence a question of redundancy. By 1792 the seamen concerned had become ac-

customed to a certain standard and mode of living for themselves
and their families, which was threatened by a sharp rise in the cost
of living. This naturally resulted in vigorous collective action in
self-defence. Prevailing assessments and expectations as to what
ought to be the proper standard of living for a certain group in
society provide in themselves a social phenomenon which can vary
markedly in time and place.

In 1815 the sudden redundancy of many seamen in the immediately post-war months sparked off defensive collective action
in much the same way as in 1792, although the cause was different.
Living in the later twentieth century, we require no very prolonged
illustration of the continuity and persistence of these particular
grounds for the emergence of industrial disputes. More generally,
the two cases also show how the origin and development of industrial disputes can be markedly affected by differing circumstances prevailing in the national or regional economy. A similar
demonstration of the connection between the prevailing economic
conditions and the climate of industrial relations is offered by the
1871 engineers' strike, where boom conditions in that industry
greatly improved the bargaining power of the workers involved.
That the connection can itself vary is implicit in the circumstances
that the 1815 strike resulted from an economic climate which
brought large-scale unemployment, and that of 1871 from a
situation in which key groups of workers were in high demand.

Another element which is commonly influential is the actual
nature of the work situation, something which varies both in its
capacity to encourage effective collective action and in the extent to
which it contributes potential causes of friction. The nature of the
early seamen's strikes owed much to the organization of the
shipping industry concerned. The dominance of the coastal coal
trade, with its short voyages and frequent return to home ports,
facilitated co-ordination among its workers. So did their social
environment, with seafaring families commonly living in their own
residential areas, with their own distinct habits and customs, which
again encouraged communal action in defence of their interests.
The high propensity of mining industries to industrial disputes,
which has often been pointed out in connection with other
countries as well as Britain, arises in part at least from similar
causes. Like the seamen, miners habitually worked together in a
context separated from other groups and lived for the most part in

mining communities dominated by this one source of employment. This separateness can be seen at work during the disputes of the 1920s, both in the highly individual course pursued by the miners and in the tenacious resistance made possible by a powerful social cohesion in the mining communities.

Other aspects of work situations could also exercise a powerful effect on the course of industrial relations, though again the effect may not be simple. Jobs which are dirty, unpleasant or dangerous present obvious opportunities for friction. Coalmining is a very clear example here. Even in the 1920s a high proportion of British coal mines had seen only very limited mechanization, and underground work involved a great deal of hard manual labour in conditions which were often repellent. Where a man is asked to risk life and limb in such conditions it is perfectly comprehensible that grievances can be felt very strongly. The outbreak of the 1970 Pilkington strike provides something of a parallel here. Working conditions in the shop where the dispute originated were distinctly uncomfortable, with a degree of heat perfectly capable of affecting the temper of those employed. Moreover, this circumstance led to a very high turnover of personnel; the Commission of Inquiry noted that three-quarters of the original strikers had worked there for less than one year, and could scarcely be expected to have a high degree of attachment to the firm and its established procedures. On the other hand industrial disputes can blow up from adverse work conditions in forms other than physical discomfort or danger, and the boredom engendered by a tediously repetitive and undemanding task can in itself provide fertile breeding grounds for discontent and restlessnes.

The extent to which the appearance of friction in any given work situation will proceed to conflict and eventually strike action will vary also markedly according to the calibre of the workers and the employers or managers concerned. It is important here to realize that a simplistic grouping of 'the workers' employed in a given setting can be highly misleading. Such a group will naturally include a considerable variety of individuals, differing among themselves in such attributes as physical and intellectual ability, powers of expression and persuasion, and degree of interest in collective activities of various kinds. In any given working context there are likely to be pervasive systems of influence within the working group, and the ideas, interests and aspirations of those who exercise influence over their fellows can have a crucial effect upon the course of industrial relations. Instances of this ascendancy occur in a number of our examples. We know tantalizingly little about the members of the strike committees which managed the seamen's side of the disputes of 1792 and 1815, but enough to recognize their superb qualities of leadership and organization, and the clear demonstration of their authority over their fellows. At this early date, however, such a high level of cohesion among large groups of workers was uncommon. It stemmed in part from the elements of work situation and community already mentioned, in part also from the fact that seafaring was an extremely dangerous occupation at that time. This circumstance had already given rise to co-ordinated activities to provide help for shipwrecked mariners and their dependents.

The strikes mentioned here were not the only contemporary evidence for the unusually high level of collective feeling among seamen. The naval mutinies of 1797 provided further instances of this. These outbreaks, which paralysed much of Britain's naval power at a crucial stage in the current war, arose from long-standing grievances about wages and conditions which, despite numerous protests, had been ignored by the naval seamen's national employer. Even here, however, events did not take a uniform course. At Spithead the men's leaders carefully confined their objectives to the grievances directly responsible for their refusal to sail, and contrived to evince a continued appearance of moderation and a desire for a peaceful solution to the problem; here the mutiny ended with an agreed programme of reforms in wages and conditions and a royal pardon for those involved. At the Nore the situation developed differently, with a much more overt challenge to existing authority and social order from a leadership willing to extend the scope of the outbreak far beyond the original grievances; this part of the outbreak ended with a series of courts-martial, which passed fifty-nine death sentences, of which twenty-nine were carried out.

The quality of leadership provided by John Burnett and his associates during the engineers' strikes of 1871 points to the significance of the informal patterns of influence and authority existing within working groups. The 1970 Pilkington strike again illustrates the way in which the course of a dispute could be markedly affected by the patterns of influence and interest among the workers concerned. The nature and the militancy of the unofficial leadership exerted a crucial impact on the course of the strike, while their opportunity was to a considerable extent derived from the lack of interest in union activities evinced by the majority of the work force for a long period before the strike erupted. The nature of the men who led the TUC during the general strike of 1926 exercised an influence on the course of that dispute far beyond that exerted by the mass of their followers, although the different qualities of many of the local leaders had much to do with the solidarity of the strike while it lasted. The three American strikes illustrate other ways in which the nature of the work force and its internal relationships could affect the course of industrial relations. In the first two examples the result was influenced by the current large-scale immigration into the USA and the lack of coherence between new arrivals and established groups of workers. The exclusiveness of the small craft unions was another important element. The third American dispute exhibited a different context, with a much more coherent posture among a more settled work force.

The nature and quality of employers and managers could equally affect the pattern of industrial relations. Since the maintenance of good relations with the relevant work force may be accounted an important function of management, it is a reasonable *a priori* assumption that the occurrence of a strike represents some failing in this key management function. We need not suppose that the need to cultivate good relations with employees is simply the fruit of the enhanced importance of workers in our modern society. It has not been only in modern times that workers have been able to exercise sanctions of various kinds against recalcitrant employers. We could usefully note how in our early seamen's strikes shipowners evinced a notable reluctance to expose themselves to subsequent reprisals by coming forward publicly to accuse strike leaders.

In our exmples of major strikes we can see a variety of instances in which employers have misjudged the situation facing them. Nevertheless the competent student of history will recognize that if he is to understand the history of industrial disputes he must make the effort to understand employers too, and not attribute to them a peculiar monopoly of human wickedness. While noting that not all shipowners agreed with him, we must try to understand how in a late eighteenth-century context, in a society which was and always had been highly unequal, Thomas Powditch could believe that negotiating with strikers was an offence scarcely inferior to rioting itself. While again noting differences of stance among the employers involved, we must try to understand why in 1871 Sir William Armstrong resisted so strenuously the notion that he should knuckle under to the Nine Hours League's demand for a shorter working week. It is perhaps even more difficult to comprehend the complexities of human behaviour which could combine in Andrew Carnegie conspicuous philanthropy with a repressive policy towards his own workers. Not all coalowners of the 1920s believed in obdurate resistance to the miners, and the position of the others must be seen in the context of the problems actually facing the industry and the nature of contemporary society, still much less affected by egalitarian concepts than the later twentieth century. When confronted with the undeniable weaknesses in Pilkingtons' arrangements for industrial relations within their empire by 1970, we must bear in mind also the complexities involved in building up such an extended enterprise and the complicated and absorbing questions of administration, production and selling which its management entailed.

A further point of importance ought to be made here. In the introduction it was pointed out that a strike is, in a sense, an inherently unusual event, and that the British record on strikes is far from being the worst among the industrial nations. We should remember that a strike which emerges wholly or in part from defective management is an event which is likely to create something of a stir and make a mark in the historical record. Where management is reasonably competent and industrial relations are reasonably harmonious, which may well be a more common situation, the continuance of normality is unlikely to be a matter of remark. In this, as in other areas of social history, it is as well to remember that the more dramatic events which erupt into public notice can often be unusual rather than representative occurrences within the society in which they take place. It is perfectly possible for many firms to experience many years of existence without serious industrial disputes; perfectly possible for very many workers to spend the whole or great part of their working lives without being involved in a strike. This does not mean that industrial relations within such a situation are necessarily idyllic, but at least the real or potential causes of friction are not allowed to erupt into a serious dispute.

Some of the ways in which the history of industrial disputes has been affected by general changes in society must also be explored. In the long span of human history the last two centuries form but a brief period, but in many ways the handful of generations involved experienced an accelerating rate of change unprecedented in earlier periods. In countries like Britain the whole scale of the national community drastically shifted. When the first national census was taken in 1801 the population of Great Britain was given as less than eleven million; by 1871 the figure had shot up to well over twenty-six million, and by the mid-twentieth century Great Britain held more than fifty million people, although by then the great period of population expansion was over. Not only had the scale of the national community shown this prodigious leap, but the distribution, employment and organization of the population had also seen unprecedentedly rapid change during the same period.

When the earliest examples of strikes given here took place Britain was essentially a decentralized rural society, even if its industrial and commercial interests were already growing in importance. By the time of the 1851 census, the majority of the people were already living in towns, even though many of these were still very much country towns. By the end of the century British society was distinctively industrialized and urbanized, with many rural areas showing an absolute decline in population. These shifts were associated with major economic developments resulting in an immense growth of production, especially in industry, together with major changes in the nature of government and the structure of the national economy.

Life in the Britain of 1792 and 1815, when our early seamen's strikes occurred, was still for most people largely bounded by merely local horizons. Industry itself was very much a local rather than a national affair, and where industrial conflicts resulted in a serious local crisis, the interference of official agencies was commonly confined to intervention by the unpaid local magistracy. The intervention of central government would only normally occur if such troubles were to threaten a serious danger to the maintenance of law and order. In any event central government did not possess the necessary resources, knowledge or understanding to enable it to embark upon any sustained course of intervention in the field of industrial relations. Society was very far from being either democratic or egalitarian. The two seamen's strikes of this period were unrepresentative in the extent of their ramifications. Not only did a major stoppage of the collier fleet threaten consequential trouble for other important elements of the local economy, such as the coal mines, but it also cut off the fuel supply to the capital and many other places. Most industrial disputes of those years had a very much more limited impact.

The transformation of British society in the course of the nineteenth century wrought great changes in such matters. The role of government, and its increasingly sophisticated resources for intervention and control, grew inexorably. The career of John Burnett, summarized near the end of chapter three, illustrated some of the early stages in the development of specialized central government agencies directly related to the course of industrial relations. By the end of the nineteenth century the Board of Trade maintained a careful monitoring survey on the frequency and extent of industrial disputes. Other expedients, such as the creation of official Courts of Inquiry into industrial disputes (seen at work in the 1970 Pilkington strike) derived from the enactment of such legislation as the Conciliation Act of 1896 and the Industrial Courts Act of 1919. In the later twentieth century, the government maintains a permanent agency for mediation in industrial disputes, ACAS, which exhibits a level of sophisticated intervention in this field which would have astonished governments of earlier periods.

The ways in which the trade union movement has developed have exhibited a parallel evolution. From very small beginnings this movement grew into one of the most powerful of national institutions, regularly consulted by governments of any party complexion. Most early trade unions were essentially local bodies, and the development of national unions paralleled the organization of other aspects of life increasingly on a national basis. As trade unions grew in size and complexity, their leaders faced problems in keeping these organizations in close touch with their mass membership, and especially with the pervasive informal pattern of shop floor leadership and influence already referred to. Many agreements on wages and conditions are now effected by general agreements between national unions and employers' organizations, but there always exists in parallel with this a great deal of entirely local bargaining and compromise related to matters actually arising

In such matters as the sharing out of overtime within a particular work situation. It is not always easy to keep these varied operations in harmony. The development of the shop steward system in the twentieth century was in part designed to bridge this often uncomfortable gap. In many unions in Britain there has also been a distinct unwillingness among many members to accept the higher subscriptions needed to equip a large national union with a staff sufficient to carry out its extended functions effectively. The circumstances surrounding the 1970 Pilkington strike provide eloquent testimony to some of these problems.

Similarly the amalgamation policy pursued by the Pilkington firm illustrates the way in which the consolidation of unionism reflected also a similar consolidation in industry, as in the emergence of such giant enterprises as ICI and GEC. Likewise provincial financial institutions increasingly gave way to national organizations such as the great joint stock banks, which swallowed up many smaller banks in various parts of the country, and further diminished the autonomy of the regional economies established in earlier stages of economic growth.

Other features which came to distinguish an advanced industrial society from its predecessors are also relevant. As dependence on ever more sophisticated products of industrial civilization grew, there was a decisive shift in the nature of social interdependence. Whereas in simpler forms of organization interdependence was common, it was frequently between people who lived and worked together in local communities, who knew each other. By the twentieth century there had been an important change here, which can be well exemplified by the development of public utilities such as water, gas and electricity, whereby whole communities, perhaps the whole nation, became dependent for the provision of essential services on small bodies of key workers, who in the nature of things must be strangers to the overwhelming majority of those they supplied. This extended interdependence has proceeded much further in the present century. The growth of the much more powerful government's control over the national economy, and the increasingly sophisticated monitoring of the nation's economic performance in relation to a world economy, has led to the situation in which the nation's health is related to the overall achievement of an aggregated production. A worker or a manager is not now simply someone who works for his own employer and lives in his own local community, but a contributor to an overall national product upon which the well-being of the whole nation can be seen as depending, including, for instance, the extent to which resources for the protection of the weaker sectors of society can be made available.

So also a worker is now very much a consumer as well as a producer, himself utterly dependent on the continuance at work of a wide variety of other specialized workers either to provide him with a specific service or more generally to maintain the health of the national economy. This is a situation radically different from that obtaining throughout the vastly greater part of history, and it imports some significant changes into the ways in which industrial disputes are approached. Moreover it is now common, though of course by no means universal, for an industrial dispute to affect the whole of a major national interest. We are now on the whole less likely to have a purely local strike of merchant seamen, for instance, with national organization and national bargaining established on both sides of the shipping industry. Industrial action by workers in the electrical power industry is unlikely to affect one area only. This increasing concentration has meant that some major twentieth-century strikes have had crippling effects on the national economy which go far beyond the confines of the industry involved. Even where the widespread dislocation which can result from a national mining strike, or seamen's strike, is not involved, the interlocking nature of many major industries can display similar repercussions. For example, the drying-up of supplies of glass for cars during the 1970 Pilkington strike threatened widespread loss of production and lay-offs in the car industry. Trends like these receive a very great deal of emphasis in modern discussion, and the 'public interest' factor involved in modern strikes is much in evidence in the treatment of industrial disputes by the mass media of communications. Again, however, it is important to remember that, while it shows some fluctuations from time to time, the British record for damaging industrial disputes is very far from being the worst among contemporary industrial nations.

A final range of considerations falls to be considered, and that is the way in which society regards itself, and the concepts of freedom in a country like modern Britain. Britain in the eighteenth century was very far from being a country in which concepts of democracy and equality had any widespread currency, yet it was also a society in which popular demonstrations of discontent were frequent. For example, riots at times of high food prices were recurring symptoms of trouble; such demonstrations were often greeted with moderation and good sense by local dominant groups. Similarly the earliest industrial disputes mentioned here demonstrate the capacity of that society to avoid unnecessary conflict. In chapter one we saw how a local magistrate could explain sensibly to a cabinet minister why it would be counter-productive to employ existing legal sanctions against miners during a strike in 1765. In our early seamen's strikes we saw examples, for which there are many parallels, of how those who held local or national power could exhibit considerable restraint in the use of repressive agencies against workers engaged in an industrial dispute which did not seem to threaten the existing order of society.

The subsequent development of British society produced on the whole a distinct movement towards the wider acceptance of concepts of freedom and democracy, though in such areas as the growth of government resources for various public objects some new forms of control could be embodied in the overall progress. This transition was in general carried out without a very great deal of internal conflict and bloodshed. This was of course a relative matter, and we should not allow the example of a pitched battle during the 1892 Homestead strike in America to inculcate too much smugness about the history of British industrial relations; in the autumn of the following year two miners were shot dead by troops during the fracas at Featherstone Colliery during a bitter miners' strike in Yorkshire. On the other hand the story of Britain during the transition to a more democratic society was a relatively peaceful one, with no major catastrophes such as the revolutions or civil wars experienced by many other nations during the same period.

The general trend during the nineteenth and twentieth centuries towards the wider acceptance of equal rights and individual freedom has had important effects in the field of industrial relations. The increased attention paid to the interests of workers has produced a legal framework very different from the older concepts of master and servant which accorded a privileged legal position to the employers. The right to strike has been regarded as an important part of the recognition of individual freedom, but there are serious problems involved in this area. It will be obvious, for instance, that the right to strike can produce situations in which the 'public interest' arguments already referred to can be in conflict with this aspect of individual freedom. Should there also be a right not to strike, or should we accept that this right of an individual can be properly constrained by the wishes of a majority of the workers involved in any given dispute? Attempts to produce a legislative framework governing the conduct of industrial disputes have not been an outstanding success, and one principal reason for this is that some of the problems involved do not lend themselves easily to legal definitions. You could, for example, try for yourself the task of framing a form of words which would adequately distinguish the point at which peaceful picketing techniques shade into coercion.

When the point has been made earlier that the British strike record is very far from being the worst among industrial countries, the basis of comparison has always been with nations which possess similar political institutions to our own. There are numerous examples elsewhere of other kinds of political systems in which industrial disputes are rare or non-existent. In such states, however, the attitudes towards individual rights and freedoms are commonly very different from our own, exemplified in the many contexts in which the existence of political groups strongly opposed to the existing order is not permitted. In general we seem to prefer our own arrangements, and the right to withdraw one's labour is an important part of the individual freedom to which we subscribe. This means that we can have situations in which groups of workers in our interdependent society can still be found taking industrial action against employers, against other groups of workers, or even in some cases essentially against the remainder of the community. Such situations can often be irritating and even damaging, but the alternatives are not especially attractive. Apart from the very grave difficulties which would in practice attend any attempt to curtail the right to strike, to do so would mark a substantial erosion of the freedom of the individual or group of workers to take action in defence of their own interests and this would mark a substantial recession from the concepts of freedom which have become established in our society over the last two hundred years.

Many of the arguments referred to here have only a limited relevance to what is likely to happen in an individual industrial dispute. It is true of course that many disputes have produced overtones of wide political or ideological implications. We have seen the youth during the 1871 engineers' strike shouting 'The Commune! Sink the damned blacklegs'; and a century later political militants seeking to intervene during the 1970 Pilkington strike. In both cases, however, the cause of the strike was something different, and it is rare for an industrial dispute in this country to have an overtly political origin. While there are many people whose personal priorities give a high and continuous place to broad political and ideological preoccupations, this is not a general feature of British society. Many workers, and for that matter many employers, are likely to concentrate more on much more down-to-earth matters of direct personal interest to themselves and their families. Industrial friction is commonly produced by such matters as working conditions, management failures in the field of industrial relations, redundancy or sharp changes in the cost of living, much more rarely by any widespread obsession with matters of politics and ideology, though it would be wrong to discount the latter factor entirely.

Finally, it should be remembered that in the origins and the course of industrial disputes we are not dealing with theoretical social categories but with the behaviour of a wide range of individuals whose immediate personal interests are involved in the limited area covered by the dispute. Broad terms like 'workers' and 'management' are likely to conceal a very considerable diversity of ideas, interests and aspirations both among those involved in a single dispute and between groups employed in differing industrial contexts. At first sight the history of industrial disputes may appear a topic which readily lends itself to generalized and simplified analysis. This might well be true if human nature and human behaviour presented us with uniform patterns; the study of industrial relations, including industrial disputes, is one area in which the complexities of human nature and human behaviour can be clearly appreciated.

Further Reading

CHAPTER ONE: INTRODUCTION

The object here is to suggest a few general books on the history of industrial relations which can help to provide a fuller background to the disputes discussed in the following chapters. A readily available book which provides a good starting-point is Henry Pelling's *A History of British Trade Unionism* (3rd ed., London, 1976), valuable for its own contents and also for its useful bibliography. Two standard works covering more limited periods are E. H. Phelps Brown, *The Growth of British Industrial Relations: A Study from the Standpoint of 1906-14* (London, 1959); H. A. Clegg, A. Fox and A. F. Thompson, *A History of British Trade Unions since 1889* (Oxford, 1964). The second and third chapters of A. E. Musson, *Trade Unions and Social History* (London, 1975) provide an important study of the development of organized labour in the second and third quarters of the nineteenth century.

As mentioned earlier, many relevant books on industrial relations have been produced by writers who are not primarily historians. From the side of law the works of Lord Wedderburn are important, especially *The Worker and the Law* (London, 1971). A convenient source for international comparisons is B. Aaron and K. W. Wedderburn, *Industrial Conflict: A Comparative Legal Survey* (London, 1972); this provides a detailed comparison between industrial disputes and systems of law in various Western countries. It was, however, written during the brief currency of the British 1971 Industrial Relations Act, and its many references to that legislation should be approached with knowledge that its life was short. For an important discussion as to the significance of strikes in modern Britain, see H. A. Turner, *Is Britain really Strike-prone? A Review of the Incidence, Character and Costs of Industrial Conflict* (Cambridge, 1969). Two books written primarily from a sociological standpoint are J. E. T. Eldridge, *Industrial Disputes: Essays in the Sociology of Industrial Relations* (London, 1968) and R. Hyman, *Strikes* (London, 1972); both of these books provide valuable ideas and information about strikes, especially in the context of recent years.

CHAPTER TWO: EARLY STRIKES

Few groups of workers have their activities in the later eighteenth and early nineteenth centuries better documented than the merchant seamen of the North-East ports, one of the major components of British shipping at the time. In addition to a wide variety of local sources from the area concerned, both the Home Office and the Admiralty papers in the Public Record Office contain a great deal of detailed evidence about these industrial disputes.

These materials have been employed by several historians, resulting in the publication of a series of articles discussing various aspects of the seamen's activities:

S. Jones, 'Community and Organization—Early Seamen's Trade Unionism on the North-East Coast, 1768–1844', *Maritime History*, vol. 3, Number 1, 1973.

N. McCord, 'The Seamen's Strike of 1815 in North-East England', *Economic History Review*, 2nd Series, vol. XXI, 1968.

N. McCord and D. E. Brewster, 'Some Labour Troubles of the 1790s in North-East England', *International Review of Social History*, vol. XIII, 1968.

D. J. Rowe, 'A Trade Union of the North-East Coast Seamen in 1825', *Economic History Review*, 2nd Series, vol. XXV, 1972.

The question of social relationships in the Britain of this period has been a topic of considerable controversy among historians, a controversy influenced by the ideological implications of the subject. For a radically different concept of the theme from that advanced here, see E. P. Thompson, *The Making of the English Working Class* London, 1963, revised ed. 1968), where the author argues for a much more pervasive situation of class conflict.

For a substantial account of the life of another labour leader of the earlier nineteenth century, see R. G. Kirby and A. E. Musson, *The Voice of the People: John Doherty, Trade Unionist, Radical and Factory Reformer* (Manchester, 1975).

CHAPTER THREE: THE ENGINEERS' STRIKES OF 1871

A principal reason why we know so much more about this 1871 strike than we do of very many other disputes is that the principal strike leader, John Burnett, wrote a substantial account of the affair immediately after its conclusion—*Nine Hours Movement. A History of the Engineers' Strike in Newcastle and Gateshead* (Newcastle, 1872). This is an indispensable source for under-standing the course of the dispute, although naturally he did not tell everything. In recent years Burnett's account has been brought together with newspaper accounts, police reports and a variety of other useful supplements in a number of discussions. The 1871 strike was considered in J. F. Clarke's thesis on 'Labour Relations in Engineering and Shipbuilding on the North-East Coast in the second half of the nineteenth century' (Newcastle University, M.A. in Economic Studies, 1966). Then the centenary of the strike was commemorated by the North-East Group for the Study of Labour History in a book *The North-East Engineers' Strikes of 1871*, by E. Allen, J. F. Clarke, N. McCord and D. J. Rowe (Newcastle, 1971). A much briefer discussion appears in the engineering section of Keith Burgess, *The Origins of British Industrial Relations* (London, 1975).

CHAPTER FOUR: AMERICAN PARALLELS

The principal sources for the three disputes summarized here are L. Wolff, *Lockout: The Story of the Homestead Strike of 1892* (London, 1965); D. Brody, *Labor in Crisis; the Steel Strike of 1919*

(Philadelphia, 1965); S. Fine, *Sit-Down; the General Motors Strike of 1936–7* (University of Michigan, 1969).

Two more general books giving a wider background are H. Pelling, *American Labor* (Chicago, 1960) and V. Vale, *Labour in American Politics* (London, 1971). D. Brody, *The American Labor Movement* (New York, 1971) is valuable not only for its own contents, but for its useful bibliography for this field. G. N. Greb, *Workers and Utopia: A Study of Ideological Conflict in the American Labor Movement 1865–1900* (Northwestern University, 1961) emphasizes some of the problems of union organization and attitudes.

Three other books are helpful in providing a more immediate background to the disputes discussed here: D. Brody, *Steelworkers in America: the Non-Union Era* (London, 1970); M. Derber and E. Young, *Labor and the New Deal* (New York, 1972); and E. Rothschild, *Paradise Lost—the Decline of the Auto-Industrial Age* (New York, 1973), especially chapters 4 and 5, which give an interesting discussion of later industrial troubles in the American motor industry.

W. H. Uphoff, *Kohler on Strike: Thirty Years of Conflict* (Boston, 1966) provides a very good example of the meticulous coverage of a complex and long-lasting industrial conflict affecting a single firm over a lengthy period both before and after the Second World War. The course and conduct of these strikes illustrate some of the points raised in the disputes already covered, and throw a good deal of light on American industrial relations and the ways in which they have changed in the present century.

CHAPTER FIVE: THE GENERAL STRIKE OF 1926

The General Strike of 1926 has attracted more attention from historians than any other industrial dispute in British history. To the books and articles already existing, the approach of the half-century anniversary in 1976 added very substantially to the material in print on this topic.

One of the most useful and readily available accounts is M. Morris, *The General Strike* (London, 1976). Another of the 'jubilee' studies is G. A. Phillips, *The General Strike: The Politics of Industrial Conflict* (London, 1976). G. Noel, *The Great Lockout of 1926* (London, 1976) is concerned mainly with the miners' strike. J. Skelley, ed., *The General Strike, 1926* (London, 1976) contributes a group of local studies and personal reminiscences. Among other useful local studies are 'The General Strike on Merseyside, 1926', by D. Baines and R. Bean, included in J. R. Harris, ed., *Liverpool and Merseyside: Essays in the Economic and Social History of the Port and its Hinterland* (Liverpool, 1969), and A. Mason, *The General Strike in the North-East* (Hull, 1970).

The tactics pursued by the government are discussed in a valuable paper by G. MacDonald on 'The Defeat of the General Strike', included in G. Peele and C. Cook, *The Politics of Reappraisal* (London, 1975). The miners' point of view was well presented by R. Page Arnot, *The Miners: Years of Struggle* (London, 1953).

The parts played by leading participants have been discussed in a number of relevant biographies. These include A. Bullock, *The Life and Times of Ernest Bevin, vol. 1* (London, 1960) and K. Middlemas and J. Barnes, *Baldwin: A Biography* (London, 1969).

An example of recent discussion of the strike from a Marxist point of view can be found in J. Hinton and R. Hyman, *Trade Unions and Revolution: the Industrial Politics of the early British Communist Party* (London, 1975).

Two variant forms of material can be added. The Sussex Tapes series of tape-recorded discussions by historians includes 'The Trade Union Movement and the General Strike', containing a discussion by Henry Pelling and Christopher Farman. The former is one of our most distinguished labour historians, while the latter is the author of another useful general account of the dispute, *General Strike, May 1926* (London, 1972). A wallet of reproduced source material, including items emanating from both national and local participants, has been produced by the Department of Education of the University of Newcastle upon Tyne; this 1971 production also includes a short history of the general strike and a commentary on the original documents reproduced.

CHAPTER SIX: ST HELENS 1970

Only three sources need be cited here; they are of different character, but complement each other in a very useful way. The first is the official report (1970) of the Court of Inquiry appointed by the appropriate minister under the Industrial Courts Act, 1919—'Report of a Court of Inquiry under Professor John C. Wood Ll.M. into a Dispute between Pilkington Bros. Ltd. (and Subsidiaries of that Company) and certain of their Employees'. Only twenty-eight pages long, the report tersely summarizes the main heads of the dispute. The second major source is the book *Strike at Pilkingtons* by Tony Lane and Kenneth Roberts (London 1971) which offers a very full account of the course of the dispute compiled by two eye-witnesses, combined with a substantial discussion of the factors involved in the strike and their significance. Together these two sources give an unusually full account of the course of the dispute and the underlying circumstances which provoked it.

T. C. Barker's *The Glassmakers. Pilkington: 1826–1976* (London, 1977) provides a full study of the company's history, with much information about the background situation to the strike.

Index